Beatitudes, Christ and the Practice of Yoga

A Sacred Log on Land and Sea

Dear Ed,
My deepest gratitude
for all your loving affirmation
and support. Fraternally!
Anthony

Fr. Anthony Randazzo
Madelana Ferrara-Mattheis

Resurrection Press
An Imprint of
Catholic Book Publishing Corp.
Totowa • New Jersey

Dedication

This book is dedicated to every person who has ever entered my classroom as a student. You have been my greatest gift in the role of teacher. Whatever I may have taught to you is only a fraction of what I have learned from you.

ℬ

In grateful memory of my mother, Marie and father, John, Aunt Margie and Uncle Rudy—they humbly lived the Beatitudes every day.

ℬ

First published in April 2006 by Resurrection Press, Catholic Book Publishing Corp.

Copyright © 2006 by Fr. Anthony Randazzo and Madelana Ferrara-Mattheis

ISBN 1-933066-00-8

Library of Congress Catalog Card Number: 2006920926

Cover design by Beth DeNapoli

Inside photos by Chara Calderone and Edward Ajaj (www.Luminawellness.com)

Printed in the United States of America

1 2 3 4 5 6 7 8 9

Contents

Acknowledgments

Our deepest thanks go to . . .

Our families:

My sisters Anna Marie and Gina, faithful sisters imitating the love of my mother.

My nieces and nephews, Marissa and Erica, David, Bobbie and Christopher. When I visited in clerical garb, David would say to me, "Where are your play clothes?" I thank the little ones for keeping me playful in the true Beatitude Spirit.

My parents, Erma and John. Mom, I see the "blessed" mother in you. Thanks for the opportunities you gave me with such an open heart. Dad, maybe this is the book you told me you would write one day.

My brother Jeffrey, my sister-in-law Joyce, my nephew Jeffrey Lee and my niece Stephanie. I cherish the depth to which our relationships have grown during the writing of this text.

My brother, Daniel and the memory of his beloved, Donna. May you both find Christ's peace in your heart.

My husband, Christopher, partner, playmate, comedic relief artist, who shows patience and love like his namesake. Thanks for believing in the light at the end of the tunnel . . . and for the lessons in home ownership!

Our professional associates and spiritual communities:

Xavier Center Staff, Convent Station, NJ; Sisters of Christian Charity, Villa Pauline, Mendham, NJ: Sr. Mary Irene, Sr. Marianne, Sr. Mary Thomas, Sr. Gail, Sr. Geralyn, Sr. Virginia; Sisters at Stella Maris, Elberon, NJ: Sr. Ann, Sr. Francis, Sr. Anne Marie, Sr. Clare. Barbara Moeller, the mother of "Christian Yoga," you are a true pioneer.

Our blessed editor: Emilie Cerar; Bon DeLuca, Dina Palmisano, Sally Ellyson, Laurette DelGuercio, and Angela Gervasio for taking the time from your busy schedules to produce, correct and comment on our drafts.

Chara Calderone and Edward Ajaj for their creative professionalism as we posed for the photos in our foldouts.

Jim McDonald, thank you for all your legal counsel.

Tom Ryan, CSP, Sharon Gannon and Baron Baptiste. Thanks for being interested in our work and supporting it with your endorsements.

Thanks to all of our friends who supported and encouraged us through this journey, with special thanks to:

Msgr. Ed Ciuba, brother, friend, pastor for his wisdom and telling me "It will be done." Msgr. Ken Herbster for his fraternal encouragement. Fr. Anthony Ciorra for believing that programs combining Christ and yoga could fly at the College of St. Elizabeth. Linda Baratte continues to believe. Fr. Tom Ryan, CSP for becoming a mentor through his work and scholarship.

Jyoti Crystal and Jason Martin for opening their arms and the doors of Starseed to nurture my growth as a yoga teacher.

Jody Domerstad for her steadfast friendship. Thanks for so generously allowing us to do our photo shoot at your beautiful studio, Become One.

Lisa Griffin, my soul sister, for jumping in the car and driving five hours to assist in our big debut!

My dear friend and spiritual mentor, Father Anthony Randazzo, who had the vision to see something in me that I could not see in myself. I am so renewed for having walked this path with you. And now my Bible travels along with my Yoga Sutras everywhere I go.

We are forever grateful to the communities of Notre Dame parish, North Caldwell, NJ; Starseed Center for Yoga and Wellness, Montclair, NJ; Become One, Rutherford, NJ; Highland Yoga, Butler, NJ; College of St. Elizabeth, Summer Institute, Convent Station, NJ; and Oak Ridge III, Mt. Paul, Oak Ridge, NJ—www.christianspracticingyoga.com—check out what open hearts and Divine inspiration can produce! Without you all, this would still be just a great idea!

And finally, to anyone who knows their name belongs on this list. We may have had a momentary bout of writer's block.

Foreword

THIS book is a creative and integrative work. It is based on the conviction that the message and intent of the Beatitudes can become clearer in our minds and experienced in our bodies through yoga postures and rhythmic breathing.

How many of the Beatitudes could you recite from memory? Here is a creative work that invites you not just to embrace them mentally but to experience them physically while simultaneously contemplating their meaning. Yoga is proposed as a dialect in what is sure to be for many a new body language of faith.

Fr. Randazzo and Ms. Ferrara-Mattheis suggest that by embodying the meaning of each Beatitude on a yoga mat, we will find an increase of support and inspiration for giving them expression in our living.

The authors are part of a growing network of Christian practitioners and teachers of yoga in the North American context (see www.christianspracticingyoga.com) who are enriching their faith lives with new (for Christians) tools of practice. As the world religions' expert Houston Smith has said, "I have a nourishing diet in my own Christian tradition, but I also take vitamin supplements."

Fr. Anthony and Madelana put certain of the yoga *sutras* in dialogue with the Beatitudes out of their conviction that the former can help us understand the latter. *Sutra* literally means "thread" in Sanskrit and refers to aphorisms which serve as mnemonic devices to connect the mind like a thread to a whole world of associations and meanings. The *sutras* encourage cultivation of a state of being marked by clarity of mind and purity of heart. Similarly, our writers work with the Beatitudes as short teachings that help us see more clearly what brings true happiness in living in community; guidelines that open our hearts to choose accordingly in the use of our time, energy and talent.

What is the meaning of this word "blessed" that is used in most translations of the Sermon on the Mount in Matthew (5:3-

12) and Luke's (6:20-23) gospels wherein we hear a teaching in Jesus' distinctive voice? When Jerome translated the Bible into Latin in the 5th century, he chose to translate the Greek word *"makarios"* with the Latin word *"beatus"* from which we get "beatitude." These words have a richer content than "happy," which risks trivializing the biblical teaching into something akin to "Have a nice day."

"Blessed" means something consecrated to or belonging to God. It came to mean in Christian use the ultimate joy, no greater gift, participation in the communion of the Holy Trinity's own life, being blessed with qualities that seem humanly impossible, and sharing in God's immortality through incarnating these qualities in daily life.

The Beatitudes do not intend to name eight different qualities as though they were alternatives that one might choose on the road to salvation. Rather, together they point to a particular type of person: the one who does not fit the secular world's idea of success. The woman who joins a not-for-profit company when she has the "smarts" to become a hard-hitting executive. The person who "wastes his manhood" on a monastery and a life of prayer. The college grad who elects to teach in the worst high school in the city.

How many people do you know who would place a higher priority on compassion, meekness, and humility than on assertiveness, self-reliance, and ambition? In emphasizing humility, dependence, and the avoidance of a spirit of self-sufficiency, what do these qualities want us to understand about life?

Surely there is nothing virtuous or blessed about poverty, hunger, and suffering in themselves. In the "blesseds" we find the insight that the needy represent the heart of the human situation. At the core of our existence is a neediness that can only be filled by God.

The spirituality underlying the "blesseds" increases our awareness that we cannot save ourselves, that neither money nor power will save us from suffering and death, and that no matter what we achieve in our lifetime, it will be less than we wanted. The Beatitudes root us in the awareness that we need God's help and mercy more than anything else.

We know that neediness in our heart of hearts, but we try to mask it rather than face it and live out of it. Life, however, continually conspires to unmask our illusions. The neediness is built in. It is not meant to be denied or run from. It is meant to turn us to God.

Someday your child may make choices that fly in the face of everything you've tried to teach. Someday you may go to the doctor not feeling well and be told before you leave that you're full of cancer. Someday a company or business you have started may go belly-up due to market forces or the decision of a conglomerate competitor to open in the same neighborhood. And then you will be face to face with your own neediness.

This is what it means to be "poor in spirit": to never lose sight of our neediness and our dependency upon God. When we are aware that we are not in control, not in a position to call all the shots, the result is a patient and humble acceptance with a steadfast heart of what happens, free from bitterness and belligerence.

This is such an important awareness to cultivate within ourselves that soaking our consciousness in it any way we can is wise spiritual practice. The practice Fr. Anthony and Madelana propose is disarmingly simple: enter into a yoga posture that expresses a "blessed" attitude of the heart and hold it, contemplate it, see what that heart-posture feels like in our body-mind. Gradually overcome our fears of it and possible revulsion for it.

Christianity has as much to do with the body as it does with the mind (the *bodily* resurrection, the *bodily* ascension, the outpouring of the Holy Spirit into these *bodies*). So it may be that we seize the wisdom of God's upside down values in an inverted position. It may be that we finally see Jesus' heavenly insight when we are face down on the floor.

Why should it surprise us that experiencing the meaning of something in our bodies through the alignment of physical posture and mental attitude would provide inspiration for our living? After a massage, we move through the day more slowly and peacefully. After a married couple make love, they arise to undertake their responsibilities from an inner space of affirmation and security.

Fr. Anthony and Madelana put before us the fruit of their own experience: Embodying the spirit of the Beatitudes through yoga postures can be a means for (re)discovering and renewing our identity as Christians. They take us on an imaginary spiritual navigation in the hope of awakening in us an attraction for the unworldly ways of the Holy Spirit. Their book exemplifies that yoga, while not a religion itself, can be used in support of religious faith.

Union with the Divine is the ultimate goal expressed by most religious traditions, though there are some important differences in our understanding of this union. Where a Hindu might say "I am God," a Christian carefully says, "I am one with God, but I am not God." What is not to be missed here, however, is that Christianity and the yogic tradition both believe that it is possible to begin living this mysterious experience of union now and to bring it to fuller awareness.

In order to move closer to the divine grace at the root of our being, the authors write, we must more fully embrace our human nature. To this end, they propose yoga as a helpful practice by which to embrace our embodied being. Through its physical and spiritual aspects, we may become like a new resident in the home of our own body-mind, learning to live with greater awareness and appreciation in every room, and creating a more hospitable and compassionate space for others in community.

For such a journey, whether on land or sea, one can only say "All aboard!"

Fr. Thomas Ryan, CSP

*Yoga must make you a lover
of the Gospel, a yogi of
Jesus Christ, true
practitioner of the
Beatitudes.*

—J.M. Dechanet, O.S.B.

Introduction

UNUSUAL matching is part of nature. Bringing things together that are normally apart and distinct can initially confuse us or make us question the association. It is not every day that a yoga teacher and a Catholic priest collaborate on a project that seems like mixing apples and oranges. Catholic priests exercise Christian ministry; yoga teachers assist students in exercising their bodies and breath. Crossing over the line from yoga center to Church and vice-versa may seem, for some, to go over the edge. Our hope is that after you experience this book, you will be entirely comfortable practicing your faith and practicing yoga.

Because the concept of this text is the blending of two distinct disciplines, much of what you will read will appear as if it were written by one. That is to say, this font will be used when the thought is the result of our individual experiences and perspectives blended into one voice. To magnify the uniqueness of our life experiences though, we will offer our individual perspectives in different fonts. To differentiate each of our voices, **this font will appear when Anthony is speaking. And another will signify Madelana's voice.**

Our experiences in life form us in new and unexpected ways. My seminary days were formal days of priestly formation. We were told that our training for ministry never ended; priestly formation was a life-long process. Enter the practice of yoga. Yoga's meaning and effect is different for everyone. Personally, the practice of yoga has made a profound contribution to my priestly life. I do not see yoga merely as an ancient set of exercises that travel on the practitioner's mastery of breathing.

Yoga was introduced into my life by chance at a health club about ten years ago. I was tired of swimming and wanted to try something different on land. I could not touch my toes, but the teacher's kind, encouraging and affirming manner persuaded me to return the following week for another class.

11

Nancy, my first yoga teacher, was patient with my stiff body and, with her assistance, I was finding that yoga was becoming a part of my life. I began to take note of physical changes, and lo and behold I was beginning to enjoy the experience despite the way the poses met the tightness of my hamstrings. The encouragement of my classmates provided me with the affirmation to continue as they noticed my improvements. They thought it was "neat" that a Catholic priest was in class with them.

As the postures opened up my body like never before, I felt myself becoming, for lack of better terms, hooked on yoga. I began to seek out and go to yoga centers. I found my way to the Kripalu Center in Lenox, Massachusetts, to follow seminars with topnotch instructors from around the country. Through the years, I have enjoyed many forms of yoga from gentle to power, from *Ashtanga* to Bikram. I have tried to expose myself to the full menu of yogic reflections and to a variety of teachers and styles. At the *Jivamukti* Yoga Studio in downtown Manhattan, I was extremely impressed with the many young adults chanting at the beginning of class. I was moved by how heartfelt the chanting sounded in Sanskrit. On another occasion an instructor played Gregorian chant during our class. The picture was getting bigger and more fascinating. Here was a Roman Catholic priest getting hooked on yoga; how strange is that? Can being a Christian and a priest be compatible with chanting "*Om?*" Madelana, my co-author, addresses that question with her revelation, "In time I began to see Anthony as a human being with a love for Christ and a love for yoga. It is that simple."

I was learning yoga with the drive and great enthusiasm of a newcomer. I discovered Starseed, a yoga center in Montclair, New Jersey. There I met wonderful teachers, particularly Jyoti Chrystal and Jason Martin, who patiently guided me as I began to integrate yoga into a regular part of my life. I met my co-author, Madelana, at Starseed. I anticipated her well-taught classes and began to understand the impact of yoga on my ministry and life. Yoga class times began to appear on my appointment calendar and soon our parish secretary, Angela, was placing my copy of *Yoga Journal* next to mail from the archdiocese. With many classes behind me, I began to notice significant changes in my body. My voice sounded softer and my soul was being given another opportunity to expand and grow within my body. Meditation and relaxation had become cherished moments of my day; yoga had begun working some of its divine effects upon me.

The most exciting benefit happened when I became aware that yoga was positively impacting my spirituality and ministry. Eureka! I have found an experience that can assist me in my on-going formation; the process of becoming more compassionate in Christ each day finds an ally in yoga practice! This was an unexpected gift coming from another world of meaning and metaphor. Downward dogs, cobras and *chatturangas* entered the zone of my soul as I ministered as a happy parish priest.

Eventually, I discovered a desire to bring together some of my passions. My primary passion is my relationship with Christ. That has been nourished through spirituality, theology and ministry. Just maybe I could take my budding passion for yoga and connect it to my theology, ministry and spirituality. The College of Saint Elizabeth, Convent Station, New Jersey, gave me the academic forum to pursue this interest. The first course I taught in which I began to unify my passions was *Christology and Christian Yoga.* "Christian Yoga" was a term I discovered in a program at Our Lady of Lourdes Wellness Center in Haddington Heights, New Jersey. Barbara Moeller's manual, *Christian Yoga: The Body at Prayer,* led me to Fr. Thomas Ryan's work on the *Prayer of Heart & Body.* All of the information was coming in rapidly; how could I process this for people today? How could I help people to be absolutely comfortable about yoga and their religious identity, specifically a Christian identity?

Talking to people at a Yoga Journal Conference about the ideas in this book encouraged me to pursue this book and to invite Madelana into the project. A yoga teacher and a Catholic priest matched together, not by chance, but perhaps by the intention of the Divine could offer a wider perspective to an interested audience. The way that Madelana experiences yoga as a woman, married person, trained teacher, baptized Catholic, is different from my experience as a male, celibate priest, Christian teacher and preacher. Joining our different world views, different life schedules, and different spiritualities around the theme of yoga is our goal.

I had been scheduling Madelana's yoga classes into my weekly schedule for some time. Would she be interested in joining me on this project? I marvel at God's-incidences—what many regard as coincidences. Yoga's classical meaning is about the practitioner arriving at an experience or multiple experiences with the Divine. In this joint project God is using a teacher and a priest for the explicit benefit of all those who wish to unite their yoga and their faith. Madelana's enthusiasm for the project confirmed for me that this project was best approached with two yogic hearts beating as one. As we embarked on this journey together, I learned her story.

I was raised as a Roman Catholic and attended eight years of parochial school. Unfortunately, my religious education did not inspire me to study the Bible, and my childhood parish left me feeling isolated and unsupported. As a child of divorced parents, my main experience of Catholicism was that we were outcasts and did not deserve to be treated with respect or kindness. In my mind, "the Church" was a political organization that did not care about parishioners who could not financially advance its position. My family was certainly not able to do that, and so we did not deserve a place in their community. At a very young age I decided that this was not how Christ would have behaved, and so I decided that I could aspire to evolve in a spiritual way that was not predicated on going to religious services or following an organized religion.

I have been practicing yoga since 1993. I began practicing with Kathleen, a friend who was teaching yoga in the health club where I worked. I had done some yoga many years earlier, but for some reason, when I began this time it seemed like I was satisfying a thirst that had long been unquenched, one that I had not even recognized having. I immediately took to this yoga experience, committing to that class every week. It wasn't long before I was asking for more yoga. Kathleen started me on a journey that has been an amazing odyssey and became the catalyst that completely changed my life. It guided and supported me through many changes. The journey that yoga has taken me on has been full of unexpected passages. Anthony's friendship and this book are but two. The writing and reflecting I have done for this project provided the opportunity for me to reconsider Christ and how the message of Christ might be present in my yoga experience.

Yoga initially came into my life as a part of my fitness routine. In the beginning, it was a purely physical experience. The systems of the body fascinate me. The wisdom and working of the body is like an ocean so deep and chock full of glorious and amazing life forms that I will never reach the bottom and I will never see them all. I quickly discovered that the physical benefits from practicing yoga were many. For me those benefits included a feeling of health and well-being, with evidence of improvements in my physical health constantly arising. From the awareness of these physical changes, I discovered that the effects could also touch my mind. I experienced more clarity in thought; I felt more self-assured and was more self-directed. When my mind became clear, like a beautiful pond in which the sediment, churned up by a storm had become still and undisturbed, I was able to see my reflection with ease. With my reflection visible on this pristine surface, the inner doubts that churned up the sediment had faded away. Yoga, it seems, was leading me to the self-acceptance that I had been searching for since childhood.

Yoga is a practice. We say we are "practicing yoga." Playing the piano requires practice. Singing a song really well requires practice. Similarly, one does not sail a fabulous yacht before practicing on a small, less expensive boat. But what are we practicing when we "practice" yoga? Yoga practice teaches us about our nature. It shows us if our tendency is to persevere or to surrender, all the while demonstrating our relationship to ourselves while we explore that process. The metaphor for all of this practice is our body. By learning when to engage and when to relax our muscles; when to play and when to use our minds; when to persevere and when to surrender with our hearts and wills, we can begin to know the true self. We may learn about our tendency to be compulsive. We may begin to discover how our analytical mind invokes tension in our physical body. We discover correlations between our habitual behaviors and the emotional expressions that accompany them. Yoga does all of this and so much more.

With a long-term committed yoga practice I began to touch the surface of understanding how body and mind reside together, but the thread that weaves the connection through them is Spirit. Spirit, the force within that speaks in a whisper; Spirit, playful and joyful and loving. When I'm in conscious relationship with Her, I am filled with a vast capacity to love. For me this is the greatest value of practicing yoga. It's in a moment of pure relaxation and effortless focus that I find Her. And that moment happens most often when I least expect it. Practicing yoga is really practicing life mindfully.

Christ taught the Beatitudes on the mount in Matthew's Gospel and on the plain in Luke's Gospel. Reconsidering the Beatitudes within the practice of yoga is creatively merging two plans of spiritual growth and development. Discovering the deeper meaning of the Beatitudes may be achieved for you as your spiritual awareness expands through a disciplined practice of yoga. Incorporating the Beatitudes on this novel journey will help us arrive relaxed at many destinations thought to be outside the scope of faith. Throughout the text you will notice small and large interconnections between Beatitudes, Christ, and the practice of yoga. On and off the mat, this text may serve as a simple guide for anyone interested in practicing faith and practicing yoga. We are using the language of Christian faith, but it is our hope that people of other faiths will feel somewhat comfortable with our text.

Yoga finds a partner with Christ. Christ lived to unify people around an all-inclusive experience of God. Reconnecting the sinful and unwanted back to God and the community steered Christ's ministry as the great and holy unifier. Yoga pursues the same kind of Christ-work joining together all in a compassionate, divine harmony. **My personal experience of Christ in prayer, coupled with yogic practice, inspires me to work for the unity of all people. Becoming one in God was Christ's goal and it is the yogic goal par excellence. When I asked Madelana to seriously reflect on Christ, she responded like this:**

"You are not a human having a spiritual experience; you are a spirit having a human experience." Though I do not know the author of this quote, it is one of my favorite sentiments. When I think about Christ, I think of a man. I think of Christ as a human being, not one with super-human powers. I think of Christ as a man who had a special mission. I think of him as being like Gandhi, like Buddha, like the Dalai Lama. I have not studied Christology and do not know more than the simple Bible stories I remember from my childhood; however, many people all over the world know of this man called Christ. We must know him because his story holds power and promise. For those who know Christ, he is a wonderful example of how one may embody compassionate and loving philosophical and ethical practices. His example is a great one and it must be studied in order to provide the best possibility for inspiration.

The following two stories "Jesus Stills the Storm" (Mt 8:23-27) and "Jesus Walks on the Water" (Mt 14:22-27) serve as inspirational guideposts for the titles of our chapters. We feel that these stories dare the listener to pay attention and offer comfort to the doubter through metaphor.

Jesus Stills the Storm (Mt 8:23-27)

And when he got into the boat, his disciples followed him. A windstorm arose on the sea, so great that the boat was being swamped by the waves; but he was asleep. And they went and woke him up saying, "Lord save us! We are perishing!" And he said to them, "Why are you afraid, you of little faith?" Then he got up and rebuked the winds and the sea; and there was a dead calm. They were amazed saying, "What sort of man is this, that even the winds and sea obey him?"

Jesus Walks on the Water (Mt 14:22-27)

Immediately he made the disciples get in the boat and go on ahead to the other side, while he dismissed the crowds. And after he dismissed the crowds, he went up the mountain by himself to pray. When evening came, he was there alone, but by this time the boat, battered by the waves, was far from the land, for the wind was against them. And early in the morning he came walking toward them on the sea; they were terrified, saying, "It is a ghost!" And they cried out in fear. But immediately Jesus spoke to them and said, "Take heart, it is I; do not be afraid."

The two focus stories we begin with from the Gospel of Matthew serve as "spiritual metaphor donors." Our metaphor of Christ is that he is the captain of our boat and a powerful being who deserves this position. This is underlined by his interaction with nature demonstrating this power. These stories give us language and imagery about the tumultuous and serene aspects of many of life's journeys. Both speak of fear, and we believe that fear is the greatest deterrent to love. In both stories, Christ is confronted by the fear of his closest friends, upsetting situations for most of us. We invite you to board our metaphorical boat and, leaving your preconceived ideas behind, allow your imagination to be free and active.

Leaving loved ones always stirs the heart. Each time I leave my relatives in Sicily, we never know if we will see each other again. There are always final waves after the kisses and the hugs. This text has many final waves from one chapter to the next. The "final waves" from one chapter usher in the "gentle hellos" of the next chapter. *Beatitudes, Christ and the Practice of Yoga,* is written with Christ as our captain, the Beatitudes as our map, and the practice of yoga as our work on board. Come with us to the dock; a new world awaits your exploration, curiosity and open spirit.

NOTE: The authors of this book are not physicians and the ideas, procedures, and suggestions in this book are not intended as a substitute for the medical advice of a trained health professional. The reader is advised to consult with his or her physician before undertaking any of the practices contained in this book. An *asana* practice should be planned according to the requirements of each person. The practice sequences may not be suitable for those with no previous experience with yoga. Regardless of your background, the help of a competent teacher is important in designing the most appropriate yoga practice for you. The reader should also consult regularly with his or her physician in matters relating to his or her health, particularly in respect to any symptoms that may require diagnosis or medical treatment. The author and the publisher disclaim any liability allegedly arising directly or indirectly from the use of this book.

Chapter 1

At Dockside with the Spiritual Navigator

SPIRITUAL development can be likened to a journey that passes through widely diverse terrain. Preparing for the array of possible events is no small feat for the traveler. Passing along a verdant valley on a warm, sunny day is quite a different experience from navigating a rocky ledge with a 100-foot drop during a storm. The road to spiritual development can present equally dissimilar circumstances with all of the accompanying challenges. For example, celebrating the gift of new life or a second chance at life are spiritual events with challenges quite different from those following a loss or a death.

In preparing for this journey, we are called upon to organize our gifts and innate qualities as well as to recognize our limitations. And when unforeseen and unpredictable challenges present themselves, the journey itself is often the best preparation. Surviving those challenges and viewing them as sacred gifts offered to strengthen us and light our way is a typical attitude for spiritual navigators.

After days, months, sometimes years of searching, spiritual navigators emerge stronger, more resilient versions of themselves. Some begin to look for a new experience of the religious faith of their childhood when, in some cases, their own child's innocent questions about God sends Generation-X parents back to their religious roots. In the Catholic tradition, a child's sacramental preparation may get parents to recall their own religious education. Others explore a variety of religious traditions, sampling different religious practices, until a particular practice satisfies something deep within the heart.

In this chapter, we will outline seven distinguishable traits of a spiritual navigator. Whenever possible, we have offered personal accounts to add further insight into these traits. Whether or not you are currently practicing a religion, try to read this book with an open mind. The words we have written are food for thought. Our intentions are not to force feed you, but to encourage you to taste something new.

The following two accounts provide examples of ordinary people acting under the guidance of their spiritual strength. These are only two such stories; we all have similar stories that tell of people who have selflessly stepped forward to navigate a person or situation to a compassionate landing.

My father was a fisherman from Sferracavallo, Sicily. He often told my sisters and me that he was "born in the sea." As children, we giggled about such an assertion. One day while at the shore I learned the meaning of that expression. While on a clamming adventure with my father and our captain, a dear family friend, the waters became rough and choppy. Seeing our captain becoming uptight and apprehensive about steering our small craft, my father volunteered to take the wheel. His "born in the sea" qualities surfaced as he navigated us safely back to the bulkhead.

As a child, our family always had a membership in the community pool. One beautiful summer day while there, my mother and I noticed a young child playing dangerously close to the pool's edge. Suddenly, he vanished! My mother leapt into action and dragged the small child out of the pool and onto a towel. The boy's father stood alarmed, pensive and paralyzed by his son's motionless body. As that little boy lay there turning blue in the face, my mother began to yell out orders to the man: "Pinch his nose and blow into his mouth!" "Again!" she yelled,

"Do it again!" Finally, after some long, tense moments, the little boy spit out a mouthful of water and began to cry. The relief among the crowd was palpable as my mother kept her cool while this man saved his son.

Our stories depended on the calm disposition and knowing, trusting action of the navigating party. Keeping centered allowed them to stay focused on what needed to be done. A spiritual navigator can be defined as an individual who has awakened to the presence and attraction of the Spirit; someone who wants to act differently in relationship to persons, places and general experiences. Certain characteristics commonly surface in spiritual navigators as they embark on life's journey.

A listing of traits describing the "spiritual navigator" would be inexhaustible. The seven traits described here simply begin our dialogue. As we refer to these traits in our text, we'll suggest ways that practicing both yoga and the Beatitudes can help reveal or develop them.

1. Enterprising Receptivity

Enterprising receptivity lays its groundwork in our childhood. A child who receives a new toy and discovers how to play with it is demonstrating his enterprising abilities. **When I was a child I would perform experiments with my Matchbox cars. Racing them down the kitchen table, I watched to see if they would stop or fall off the edge. Would other cars produce the same result?** As children, what we do with a particular toy is more a function of our enterprising spirit than learning to follow instructions on a box. The more a spiritual navigator can retain this child-like trait, the more effective their spiritual life will be as they enter adulthood where no instructions are issued.

Little did our friend Gerry realize the harm that witnessing the constant bickering that accompanied the breakdown of his parents' marriage would have on his future relationships.

Gerry developed the preconceived notion that conflict within a loving relationship is the sure path to the end of that relationship. Without a reliable map to chart this territory, conflict in his relationships would either be avoided at all costs, or would stir up unconscious feelings, causing him (and his partner) extraordinary stress.

As a spiritual navigator, Gerry sought out new pathways for conflict resolution in his own marriage. His receptivity ensured that he considered many options in an open-minded and welcoming manner. In this way he became a witness to his own ability to learn about himself through his marital conflicts, as well as to deepen his relationship, rather than seeing conflict as a prelude to demise. Whether enterprising receptivity reshapes our use of an unpleasant childhood experience or helps us with our current relationships, the ultimate consequence is that it keeps us fully alive for new experiences. *Beatitudes, Christ and the Practice of Yoga* invites the spiritual navigator to exercise this trait to a new connection, where yoga sets the stage for living like Christ.

2. Curiosity-driven Spirituality

A common trait among spiritual navigators is an innate curiosity about so-called spiritual things. In today's world where "new-age" bookstores are popping up on every corner, it's a pretty big cookie jar, and the spiritual navigators just can't seem to keep their hands out of it. So many new terms and practices are showing up on our spiritual radar screens. What's for real? What's for me? What does the Church say?

Spiritual navigators are ceaselessly spiritually curious. You bought this book out of curiosity about how the Beatitudes, Christ and yoga fit together and if it's a match for your personal spirituality. Your journey with this book will be empowered by such curiosity. Your questions about the Beatitudes will get you excited again about your relationship with Christ through your practice of yoga. Accepting yoga as a spiritual practice in its own right will drive your curiosity to explore healthy practices and rituals that support your faith. The ultimate intention is to deepen your personal connection to the Divine within.

Spiritual practices and religious rituals are encouraged in a free society. Catholics revere the domestic tradition of a new house blessing. **When I am invited to "bless a house," I am always amazed at the curiosity of the inviting family. "What will Father do when he blesses our house?" The curiosity of the family is happily satisfied by the recitation of simple prayers and the sprinkling of holy water.**

Houses of worship receive many visitors to admire the architecture and to witness their rituals. When I visit a house of worship other than a Roman Catholic Church, I am curious about the ritual dynamics. On a recent visit to a Hindu temple, a fellow parishioner and I were extremely curious to see the priests perform rituals with water and coconut milk before a large statue of a deity.

What drives the spiritually curious person? For many, it is the desire to bond with a significant other. For example, a devout Catholic (Sheila) may develop a deep friendship with someone who practices shamanism (Rose). As a result of this friendship and her enterprising and receptive nature, Sheila may attend a sweat lodge with Rose. This Native American ritual ceremony generally involves a theme that is discussed by a facilitator before participants enter an outdoor structure heated by fired, hot rocks, to meditate and literally sweat out the theme-related toxins. Sheila could very possibly experience a profound, physical and emotional release as a result of the intense and unfamiliar nature of the sweat lodge. Sheila's Christian faith is in no way threatened by her attendance at the sweat lodge, although her emotional state may respond to "the sweat" and she may feel spiritually purified and more able to offer her unencumbered self to her volunteer work in her parish.

Wherever your spiritual curiosity may lead you it is important that you find yourself in a place within that is closer to God. Your spiritual practices and rituals should make you more open to giving and receiving love so that when you are called to serve others you feel ready and willing to answer.

3. Living with a Sense of Values

What one holds spiritually sacred or worthwhile for life is dependent upon many things, among them are family traditions, religious and moral beliefs, childhood experiences, and cultural backgrounds. Living with values allows the spiritual navigator to remain rooted in their various communities. Spiritual navigators recognize how the clarification of values leads to harmonious living, and while being true to their own values, they do not pass judgment on anyone else's values.

But what purpose do these values serve? What is the value of peace and why would I want to become a Beatitude peacemaker? Without an "awareness of values" we would trek aimlessly through life. Values keep the spiritual navigator socially aware of the wants and needs of all people, especially the need to feel secure as a family and a nation. As a society of consumers we are conditioned to place value on things. Human beings can be viewed as utilitarian and expendable. How many times do we see computers in the workplace treated better than the people who operate them?

As a certified public accountant I was absolutely miserable. I never felt that my work brought joy or happiness into my client's lives. That ability was something I highly regarded. Despite years of academic training and the subsequent study and time it took to attain those three letters (C.P.A.) behind my name, I gave it all up to pursue something that I loved. After only months of practicing yoga, I knew it was exactly what I had been looking for. I believed that financial security would naturally follow doing what I excelled at and loved. By taking a risk and being willing to fly, I was catapulted into yoga.

It was my sense of values that drove me to ask for more from my life. It was those very values that brought me to yoga, and that one step caused a wonderful chain reaction in my life that has brought me to this very day to share my journey in the book you are holding in your hands.

The Beatitudes propose values that become more discernible through the practice of yoga. Each Beatitude opens the discussion on a particular value. This book will help you to learn about these values not through your mind, but through your body.

4. "At Home" with the Inner Life

Dorothy in the *Wizard of Oz* repeated over and over again, "There's no place like home. There's no place like home." She knew deep down the comfort level of Kansas. The spiritual navigator is no stranger to the comfort zone of the inner life. The "welcome mat" is always out for the phrase, ritual, or gesture that will make them feel that God their mother has just baked their favorite apple pie; the aroma alone makes them feel quite at home. The practice of yoga broadens the spiritual navigator's at-home disposition with the inner life.

Yoga helps bring body, mind and spirit into balance. After practicing yoga for a while, you become aware of the smallest thing that disturbs this balance. It can be the slightest sign of a cold coming on or a judgmental thought that enters your mind, whatever it is your body will tell you it's not in Kansas anymore. This early detection system can sometimes prevent further injury to your body, mind or spirit.

The inner life can at times feel like a comfortable place of retreat from the chaos and demands of day-to-day life. Spending time with your spirit is like visiting an old friend. And like an old friend, your spirit is always there to look out for your best interests. When someone says, "Listen to your heart," what they are really saying is listen to your spirit.

It was not until I met my husband that I discovered the truth about creating an inner home for myself. Despite an exciting and passionate beginning, my husband-to-be needed more time to be a bachelor. After several on-again, off-again rounds, we decided to "call it quits." It was during this very dark time in my life, being without the man I really loved, that I finally found out how valuable all of the practices I was learning through yoga and meditation could be. I felt very alone, but my spiritual journey was about to take a fortuitous turn. I discovered my "true self" and, through the spiritual practices of yoga and meditation, along with a wonderful support network of friends and family, I cultivated my inner space. It was after I entered an interior place of peace and acceptance that my husband and I decided we did not want to be apart. Today we are happily married and working steadily in creating a home together. My inner home led me to my outer home.

Not always a peaceful place, the inner world can bring spiritual navigators face-to-face with some of their not-so-desirable characteristics. Coming to know our true self requires an honest approach to self-inquiry. By acknowledging our faults we can begin to change, shedding that which doesn't serve our higher self in order to reveal our more Christ-like self.

The Beatitudes, together with the practice of yoga, offer a sense of at-home comfort, particularly as the inner shadows fall on the landscape of the soul. Your present home, job, relationship, body, will take on a new feeling of security as you learn to slip into your authentic self through your work with *Beatitudes, Christ and the Practice of Yoga*.

5. Faith and Religious Faith

Alan Reder's article in the April 2001 issue of *Yoga Journal*, "Reconcilable Differences," astutely asks, "If yoga clashes with your faith, how do you work out joint custody of you? If you are trying to patch together a personal spirituality from your religion and yoga, where do you place the seams?" After September 11, 2001, many people turned to religious services and yoga classes; both experiences welcomed hurting people seeking answers. For many, the seams dividing religion and yoga faded.

Spiritual navigators are open to the language of faith or religious faith. A comprehensive approach to healing comes in the form of a "faith prescription" by Dr. Bernie Siegel. His books welcome people to experience faith in self, treatment, doctor and God. Such a "faith prescription" heals without well-defined dogmas. Consequently, faith in this context is not weighed down by religious authority and rules. For many spiritual navigators the content of a particular religious belief system is intimidating. Theological terms give way to misunderstanding and fear. In the end, the act of believing and the experience of the Divine prove more powerful than the correct vocabulary of faith.

"I am more spiritual than religious," is the self-description I often hear as a priest, coming from a person who wants to reassure me that we are in the same ballpark in matters of the spirit, but when it comes to that "religion stuff," we are different.

Such was my experience:

Yoga filled the void in my heart that was long vacant from the faith of my childhood. Repeated disappointments over a lack of support offered to my family by the leaders in my Catholic community led me to rebel against religious conscription. I witnessed some Catholic nuns and priests acting anything but spiritually benevolent toward others. I yearned for a more loving atmosphere than what I was experiencing in Catholicism.

Growing up in a particular religious faith leaves certain "soul indentations" that don't easily fade with the passage of time. Ask anyone about his or her religious identity; they will usually name some organized religion, even if they dismiss the religious practices of the denomination. *Beatitudes, Christ and the*

Practice of Yoga hopes to guide the spiritual navigator back to a healthy religious identity if that identity has become hazy.

On the topic of religious identity, I observe in my yoga students that for long periods of time, they may appear in class and never reveal anything more personal than their name and the fact that they have a chronic case of sciatica. Religious affiliation rarely becomes a topic for discussion. This book project has helped me to appreciate that many of my students do have a religious identity. I teach from a deeply spiritual, non-denominational perspective because I would never want a student to feel that religious faith or lack thereof is a reason to not practice yoga. Their desire for peace of mind and heart transcends a particular religious affiliation.

Yoga classes nationwide are drawing people who feel disenfranchised and betrayed by organized religion. Many Catholics tell stories about the "straw that broke the camel's back." These stories range from issues surrounding clerical sexual abuse to changes in the Catholic Mass. Those who have been wounded by Church laws or its representatives don't heal overnight. Is it a lack of religious faith or disappointment in Church leadership that causes alienation? Whatever reasons you may have for being alienated, yoga can be the means through which your religious identity will be renewed and rediscovered—on the foundation of the Beatitudes.

You may be totally comfortable practicing your religious faith and practicing yoga. You may be a part of a growing group that pray "Amen" on Sunday and chant "*Om*" on Monday. If so, this book will encourage you to take your faith into deeper waters.

Faith and religious faith are not strangers in the yoga world. Gary Kraftsow, author of *Yoga for Wellness*, corroborates our thoughts by taking the position, "Yoga is non-sectarian; it helps one rediscover faith." And in *Yoga: The Spirit & Practice of Moving Into Stillness,* Erich Schiffmann explains, "Yoga enhances your experiences of life. It changes your perspective, enabling you to embrace a larger, more accurate conception of who you are, how life works, and what God is."

Our text will take you on a unique kind of journey that sends you back to a pure faith where Christ is at the center teaching you the Beatitudes as you do your yoga.

6. Resilience in the Face of Challenge

Resilience keeps the spiritual navigator sailing forward on the waters of spiritual depth. In his *Currents of Grace: The Philosophical Foundations of Anusara Yoga, Vol. 1*, Dr. Douglas Brooks, Professor of Religion at the University of Rochester in New York, and one of the world's leading scholars of Hindu Tantrism, defines *challenge* as *an event that offers an opportunity to reveal more of the true self.* That unveiling of the true self involves pain of some kind; the greater the challenge, the greater the accompanying pain. Most of the time, the spiritual navigator springs back from the challenging moments, seeks healing for the pain, and reflects upon the lessons learned. The following example shows how resilience on the yoga mat may help us identify seedlings of this trait within ourselves.

I had been practicing yoga for about two or three years and had gradually advanced, with my teacher Jyoti's encouragement, into more challenging classes. I remember doing my handstand practice one evening before I was teaching a class as a student watched me. Each time I would attempt to go up, I would land back on the ground; however, I never thought I was failing. I truly expected one day to accomplish my first handstand. After watching me try, my student admiringly said, "That is true persistence." She was so validating and complimentary about the way that I just did it and did not get flustered or disappointed or critical of myself. I believe that the resilience which sustained my efforts existed long before the challenge of handstand. A simple physical act of a yoga pose clarified for me the resilience I see not only in other areas of my own life, but in the qualities my students display.

Challenge-free living is not the path advocated by the Beatitudes. All nine Beatitudes, in practice, require resilience. In a world wrought with violence, the challenge presented in the call to be a peacemaker is great. Promoting new initiatives for peacemaking requires resilience, particularly when many reject the initiative as "pie-in-the-sky" thinking. As Madelana's testimony proves, some yoga poses may actually help cultivate resilience which translates into patience and perseverance when dealing with life's major issues and tasks.

A remarkable example of resilience in our times was demonstrated to us by people who attended numerous 9/11 funerals. Civil servants went from one town to another to pay respects to colleagues, friends and strangers. Certainly, the sacred combination of faith and resilience was part of what kept them showing up to support the family and friends of the fallen. This trait within the spiritual navigator doesn't always gain proper attention and recognition. I'm sure that those who went to so many funerals never realized that they were "bouncing back" each time from a deeper part of their spiritual identity. They were giving all of us a "living witness" to the Beatitude, "Blessed are those who mourn, for they shall be comforted."

These six traits lay the groundwork for the "mother" of all spiritual traits, "being in awe of the same God."

7. In Awe of the Same God

Spiritual navigators celebrate humanity's experience of God. Where conversations about God break down because of different belief systems, the navigator listens for words about one's experience of God. Those words inspire the navigator to claim that no one group has exclusive rights to the "real God." September 11, 2001 ushered home how we all appeal to the same God. Being in awe of the same God unites the human family in a never-ending bond of pure love. We are all interconnected as we stand in awe of the one divine power and presence.

Dialogues of all kinds have hope of beginning when people start with God-experience talk before God-definition talk. The spiritual navigator, spearheading such dialogue, steps into the role of "spiritual diplomat." Imagine for a moment if all our stellar spiritual navigators took part in dialogues working for the end of poverty, "the greatest weapon of mass destruction," according to Dr. James Forbes, the Senior Minister of Riverside Church in Manhattan. Let's take our imagination further and place our renowned spiritual navigators from all religious traditions together with political leaders for a world summit on war and peace. Celebrating the common awe of the same God can literally save the world from our own self-destruction. When disagreements become unmanageable on the world stage, our "spiritual diplomats" offer the great wisdom of the Beatitude, "Blessed are the pure in heart, for they will see God."

Awakening the pure in heart is all about awe. We hope our readers will become attuned to the phenomenon of what it truly means to be in awe of the same God. As more people celebrate being children of God in awe of God's love, peace-making becomes more than just a word, it becomes a tangible reality in today's world.

~~⌒

Throughout the text, these seven traits will appear for further reflection as we sprinkle them throughout like holy water. By observing their presence in your own life, your current spiritual journey will be launched in a new and exciting direction. We will equip you with a set of navigation tools for anchoring you during times of spiritual tumult and for lightening the load when your baggage gets heavy. Happiness or blessedness on this journey reveals itself when one begins to let go, surrendering to God's plan. The "fun" is in going with the flow, the Spirit's flow.

Christ is the captain of our vessel. Reconnecting with Christ as a teacher, finding the deeper meaning of the Beatitudes and practicing yoga is the winning triad of our work. *Bon voyage*, happy to be with you on the journey.

Chapter 2

Setting Sail with Christ the Yoga Teacher

CHRISTIAN theologians say and write many things about Christ the man and his message. Jacques Dupuis, S.J. offered a verbal souvenir about Christ in a theology class at the Gregorian University in Rome that repeats itself frequently in my mind as I introduce people to a deeper relationship with Christ. "Help people fall in love with the human Jesus of the New Testament, then they will find the divine." I have quoted that line in homilies, lectures, and conversations as a means of connecting listeners with Christ through the sacred experience of falling in love. When was the last time you fell in love with something so human about Jesus? Can you remember a comment from a preacher that threw you "head over heels" about the actions and words of Jesus? After reading or listening to a favorite Gospel story, do you feel closer to God? Before you answer these questions, consider Madelana's personal testimony about falling in love.

Initially, falling in love can render us powerless. I would describe it as the sensation of tumbling through space. We are not comfortable with such strong feelings of being out of control. In general, we tend to deny, ignore, and repress our feelings most of the time. So to be spilling over with emotion like the effervescent foam on a cold, crisp beer must be attributed to the other.

My favorite description of falling in love comes from a wise teacher called Ram Dass, the author of the renowned book, *Be Here Now*. Born Richard Alpert, Ram Dass was given this spiritual name (Servant of God) in the 1960s by his spiritual guru, Maharaj Ji. He has described falling in love as *"stepping into the space of love with another."* Ram Dass' suggestion is that we can literally enter the space of love, the most powerful emotion on the planet as we would enter a room, by simply stepping in. What I appreciate about this definition is that it opens the gateway to love and all its possibilities. We can fall in love with a significant other, but we can also experience love that is not romantic love. For instance, mothers and fathers fall in love with their newborn babies every day. By being so completely influenced by the presence of that other being in our life, we are drawn deeper into our own emotional potential.

Falling in love with the human Jesus is entering the space of love with the noble desire to meet Jesus as he is described and depicted in the New Testament. Dupuis' affirmation of humanness gives us permission to find Jesus in our own ordinary human experiences. Our starting point is not an esoteric doctrine, unintelligible and removed, but a real-life experience like falling in love. Falling in love with aspects of Jesus' humanity calls us to a new appreciation of the child whose Jewish parents fell in love, loved him and taught him the Jewish faith and practices. He eventually taught in the synagogue where his parents participated in worship services. Falling in love with their son complimented the oneness of love with his heavenly Father.

Of all the descriptions I have ever read about Christ in theological textbooks, none have helped me to fall more in love with Christ's humanity than the one found in Catherine Mowry LaCugna's widely studied text, *God for Us*. Her description of Jesus encourages us to see him as a teacher of a body-oriented spirituality—for our purposes—a yoga teacher.

Jesus experienced all the drives and ambiguities of bodily existence: from thirst, sex, hunger and need for sleep, to doubt, fear and longing, suffering, and finally death itself.

Mary's adolescent body gave birth to an infant who she nursed and diapered. The Gospel of Luke confirms that the embodiment of Spirit within Jesus, "increased in wisdom and in years, and in divine and human favor" (Lk 2:52). His adult status as a rabbi followed the normal steps of human development among his peers. He made friends with males and females and experienced the sexual awakenings of puberty like every Jewish teenager. As a pre-teen, his predilection toward teaching surfaced when he amazed teachers with his wisdom in the temple (Lk 2:46). His developing male body felt pain of all kinds, his psyche felt mental anguish, and his soul's longing for the Father throughout his life was insatiable.

The Human Jesus

When we look back at our first yoga class we remember wondering, "Can I do this yoga stuff?" After that first class, we thought,"Can I ever do those poses?" Our doubts can prevent us from doing and trying new things. Christ's doubts and fears did not keep him from teaching new things about God's love and action in everyday life. Jesus broke with tradition and took risks on many occasions—reaching out to the outcasts in his public ministry. The popular story of the Multiplication of Loaves and Fish (Jn 6:1-15) shows his remarkable care for those who traveled to be fed—physically and spiritually. He was compassionate and as such, had a felt sense of their needs and fed their deep hunger and thirst. He did not stand on ceremony; his only desire was their well-being— "making the people sit down" (Jn 6:10). His pressing concern was for everyone to be equipped for the arduous journey of life. They left that miraculous meal with less fear about God and little doubt about this special man's attention to their basic needs.

To be human in the company of such an exceptional human, Jesus, gives a new awareness to being "Christ-like" in every way from the top of our heads to the tips of our toes on a colorful yoga mat. Christ could certainly be called "down to earth." Christ experienced the limitations of his own body, even though as LaCugna writes: "He was remarkably unanxious about the basic needs of survival, or about his reputation."

How was Jesus able to attend to the constant demands he encountered? He was known to retreat into the silence of the desert (wilderness) to spend time alone with his heavenly Father. One morning that deserted place caused his disciples to feel anxiety about his whereabouts (Mk 1:35-37). Before his final days, the Mount of Olives became his spiritual refuge at night and proximate preparation for the most trying days of his life. Mel Gibson's *The Passion of the Christ* gives viewers a dramatic Hollywood perspective of Christ's prayer life in Gethsemane where his major concern was about his imminent danger and death.

Absolute trust in God as his loving Father (Abba) gifted his peripatetic ministry with a healthy disregard of others' judgments. His opponents, Pharisees (astute lawyer-types) and Sadducees (powerful political-types) felt his reputation was constantly being tarnished by the company he kept—people with poor reputations like tax collectors often dined at table with him. He said and did things that traditional rabbi-types of his time simply did not dare to do. In the end, his reputation as the so-called "King of the Jews" was firmly rejected by him. He was much more comfortable with those who compromised his reputation, like lepers and prostitutes, than with building his good name in the superficial company of civic and religious authorities.

Beatitudes, Christ and the Practice of Yoga will constantly be introducing a Christ who seems like someone you already know or someone you can't wait to know more about on or off a yoga mat. Dupuis and LaCugna have hopefully guided us to appreciate that the Christ we speak of from history walked on the earth and not above it. Let's bring this first-century man on board with us into the 21st century.

Before we certify Christ as a yoga teacher for our unique journey, we applaud and accept his tenure as a renowned, spiritual teacher whose ethical teachings have fashioned Western culture.

Hanging on my bedroom wall is a Russian icon of Christ, the teacher, given to me by a dear friend one Christmas. Recently I noticed that the fingers of Christ's right hand looked like a *"mudra"* in the yoga world. I asked Madelana to interpret the fingers in her way without biasing her about their traditional, Christian interpretation.

According to my Monier-Williams Sanskrit English dictionary, *mudra* is defined as "a seal or any instrument used for sealing or stamping; the stamp or impression made by a seal." In common language, a *mudra* is a gesture made with the hands or body that leaves an impression. Its meaning is the impression that is imbedded in one's heart by the intention of the one practicing the *mudra*. Think of a *mudra* as a kind of yoga practice of the hands.

At first it can be quite challenging to practice a particular *mudra*. The simple act of touching certain fingers together in specific ways can challenge even the most avid of yoga practitioners. What is of particular interest to me when I observe the plaque of Christ with the thumb of his right hand touching the tips of his ring and pinky fingers, the other two fingers outstretched, is the gracefulness of the artist's depiction. This apparent *mudra* does have a very specific name and meaning as described by Gertrud Hirschi in *Mudras: Yoga in Your Hands.*

Called *Pran Mudra* or *Life Mudra*, the meaning of this gesture is to activate what we yogis call the "root chakra," which correlates to the tailbone and pelvic floor. Considered to be the root of our earthly being, this area is our connection into the earth like a plant that has its roots in the earth. Yogis believe that practicing *Pran Mudra* can help to nourish our vitality—our energy for living life to its fullest. Interestingly, it can also reduce nervousness and improve vision.

Nourishing the root of our being gives us a greater stability, self-confidence and perseverance. As I contemplate Christ's role and fate, I see *Pran Mudra* as a natural gesture for he who walked such a challenging path with graceful stability, confidence and vision.

Conjuring up the image of Christ as a yoga teacher (a teacher of divine union) starts as we elaborate on four gospel-based images. Remember these images each time you roll out and press down the four corners of your yoga mat. Understand that these images are complimentary of each other and distinctively mark what people remember about our Galilean rabbi. These images and our stories will bring the Yoga Teacher of the Beatitudes to life for you.

Insightful Jewish Storyteller

Middle Eastern cultures revere and hold sacred the oral tradition. That which is transmitted from one person to another through the power of the tongue is not to be taken lightly. Friendship is started and revenge carried out by word of mouth. A man's word makes him honorable or dishonorable before his family, friends and business associates. The spoken word about a person or event gets passed down, and over time the oral tradition is sometimes written down. What we know about Christ came first from Jewish oral tradition that included information about his words and deeds. The four Gospels considered collectively provide us with a composite written tradition about Jesus, as personally and spiritually insightful as traditional Jewish storytelling.

Passing on stories from one generation to another was and is legendary in Jewish culture for maintaining family heritage, religious customs and values. Christ inherited the Jewish rabbinical knack of telling a good story in his native Aramaic; (Mel Gibson's *The Passion of the Christ* gave us the sounds of this Hebrew dialect.) The term *parable* is used for his story-telling style. In fact, Mark states that he "taught them many things in parables" (Mk 4:2). Three parables: The Parable of the Lost Sheep, The Parable of the Lost Coin and The Parable of the Prodigal Son and his Brother found in Luke's Chapter 15 are often considered to be the core of Jesus' storytelling repertoire. Many authors name this trio of parables a "mini-gospel."

Perhaps, the most widely known of the three is that of The Prodigal Son. Henri Nouwen, a great teacher of Christian spirituality, creatively brought the parable to life for people of all religious backgrounds. In his popular text, *The Return of the Prodigal Son: A Story of Homecoming,* he refers to Rembrandt's painting "The Return of the Prodigal." The reader learns about the emotional make-up of each character beginning with the younger son, then elder son, ending with the father. Nouwen himself identifies with each character and asks his reader to do the same. Upon completing the book, one has gone full circuit with all the issues involved with broken relationships and their gradual healing. The parable is the perfect example of how our Insightful Jewish Storyteller invited his first audience: tax collectors, sinners, Pharisees, and scribes (Lk 15:1-2) to see themselves and their personal issues in the imagery and characters of the story.

In imitation of the Insightful Jewish Storyteller, we now offer our own stories about Christ entering the yoga world in many disguises.

Blessing Space

Once upon a time a yoga studio opened up in Manhattan. The director of the studio felt a blessing would give the studio "divine insurance" for many years. Looking out at traffic on Fifth Avenue, she noticed a man in Franciscan robes slowly walking by. In one quick moment, she ran down two flights of stairs and out the front door, chasing after the man in brown robes. Because he walked so slowly, she caught up with him in no time. After a brief introduction, she popped the urgent question: "Would you take a moment to bless my yoga studio?" Surprised at the request, the humble Jesus obliged her. He removed his sandals, walked into the yogic space, and said, "*Shantih* to this place and all that enter here." After a few more prayers, he moved his right hand from top to bottom then left to right making a cross. Then he said, "Peace to this place and all who rest here." He left, explaining to the director that when anyone asks for a blessing, peace comes, too. She profusely thanked him, and as he went on his way she prepared to teach her afternoon class feeling an inner peace in a well-blessed sacred space.

A New View

One day Jesus stopped his disciples after a long day filled with lots of preaching and teaching. He told his disciples, "We have walked for miles. We have been on our feet for hours; it is time to rest." The disciples lay down on the grass. They stretched out their legs and arms, closed their eyes. A few birds on distant trees chirped. They all faded away to dreamland. After a short snooze, they woke up, refreshed. Upon waking, they looked over and saw Jesus standing on his head in a headstand. "Wow!" Peter said. Coming gently down from the headstand, Jesus said, "We will turn the world upside down with compassion."

"As Is" Acceptance

As yoga became increasingly popular, another new studio was opening in the area. Jesus happened to walk by and noticed a sign on the window looking for teachers. When he walked into the studio space and met the proprietor, it was evident to her that this would be a very special teacher. Her goal was to reach the not-so-flexible, not-so-strong, not-so-athletic people that she felt were missing out on the benefits of yoga. She offered Jesus an immediate opportunity to audition in her 9 a.m. class and he accepted. When he walked into the room, there were 25 people waiting for a yoga class. They were young and old, male and female, a few were pregnant and one man had crutches and a cast on his leg. Clearly this was an atypical American yoga class. At that moment, the proprietor had to leave the room for a phone call and when she returned 20 minutes later, she was stunned and impressed to see that Jesus had arranged the room with every student's needs attended to. With some on chairs, some standing and two even lying down on the floor practicing breathing exercises, Jesus had accepted the condition of his students and provided individually what each one needed.

Humble Servant-like Teacher

Serving and teaching are twin functions in the Jesus story. Above all other stories showing Jesus serving people, one remains the all-time hallmark of humble service. Every Holy Thursday in the Catholic Church this story is proclaimed in its entirety and followed up by a moving foot-washing ceremony.

> After he had washed their feet, had put on his robe, and returned to the table, he said to them, "Do you know what I have done to you? You call me Teacher and Lord and you are right, for that is what I am. So if I, your Lord and Teacher, have washed your feet, you also ought to wash one another's feet. For I have set you an example, that you should do as I have done to you." (Jn 13:12-15)

In Jesus' time teachers did not perform the duties of servants. Normally, a servant was assigned by his master to extend the hospitality of foot-washing to guests upon arrival at their master's home. The dirt from dusty roads needed to be washed away before they reclined at table. Servants were possessions of wealthy owners and therefore were asked to do that which was most demeaning like foot-washing. For a teacher like Jesus to suddenly stoop down for a foot-washing crossed the boundaries of acceptable behavior for a respected rabbi. What kind of teacher acted like a slave? One who we already know was not the least bit concerned about his reputation.

By trespassing on the cultural expectations of a teacher, Christ redefined the meaning of teacher. Not only would this teacher teach with parables by the "spoken word," but he would also teach by example. The old adage, "Actions speak louder than words," applies to Christ's teaching method. In the case of the foot-washing, the disciples were being asked to learn something about selfless service even as they struggled with the awkward nature of the action coming from a teacher. If they were to become teachers in his name, they had better be ready to serve in every way, even if that meant performing the servile task of foot-washing. Anyone who decided to follow this teacher must be willing to serve humbly in respect and honor of the teacher who came not to be served but to serve.

At this time, call to mind those people in your life who remind you of the humble servant teacher. Have you met this kind of teacher in a classroom or yoga studio? Would you say most of the teachers who have taught you were humble servant teachers like Christ? Did you ever witness a teacher doing an action that showed pure service, an act that went beyond what most teachers would do for their students?

I see my co-author Madelana as a fine example of a servant-teacher in the yoga world. She never shies away from serving the individual needs of her students' bodies. She understands the limitations students bring to class. She does all that she possibly can to help her students grow in the yogic journey. Gentle adjustments that serve the integrity of the pose are given carefully and skillfully. Madelana's students would feel very comfortable if Christ were a substitute for her class. Christ's plan book and hers would include the same material. Her humble heart and Christ's

heart are coming out of that same place of sacred welcome, where wholistic wellness for students is a central concern.

The Welcoming Teacher of Sacred Relaxation

> Come to me, all you that are weary and are carrying heavy burdens and I will give you rest. Take my yoke upon you and learn from me for I am gentle and humble in heart, and you will find rest for your souls. For my yoke is easy and my burden is light.   Mt 11:28-30 (The Son's Prayer)

Andrea Bocelli and Celine Dion in their famous duet, "The Prayer," sing: "Let this be our prayer, when we lose our way, lead us to a place, guide us with your grace to a place where we'll be safe." The last part of Christ's personal prayer to the Father shares the same intention and hope of "The Prayer"— certain guidance by divine companionship to a safe place of repose.

One must feel welcomed by the divine to accept an invitation to restful waters. "Come to me" cannot be more welcoming. This invitation to others, offered by the Son who experiences intimate union with the Father, authenticates every aspect of the welcome to divine companionship. Two aspects of welcome are most significant for the Welcoming Teacher of Sacred Relaxation. One is being welcomed for the first time into a new life setting; the second is being welcomed back after being away from home. Three personal stories helped us to understand the nuances of a Christ-like style of welcome leading to "soul respite."

Christ's style of welcome reminds me of my very first yoga class. Nancy, my yoga teacher, was a master at the art of welcome, greeting her beginner and experienced students and helping them to get situated on their mats. I kept returning to that class because I felt welcomed in her yoga space. Feelings

of bodily inadequacy concerning certain poses quickly vanished. After some time the feelings of relaxation that began in her class followed me into my priestly life.

Another first-time welcome made an equally deep impression in my life. After almost ten years with an outstanding pastor and personal friend, Fr.Joseph Masiello, I left a community I loved very much. On the day I was leaving Our Lady of Mercy in Jersey City, NJ for the drive to Notre Dame, after embracing my dear friend, Fr. Michael O'Grady, I got in my car and led the movers to North Caldwell. As soon as I pulled into the driveway of the rectory, I saw a huge white sheet across the garage with the words, "Welcome Fr. Anthony to Notre Dame." Welcoming balloons were at the door and huge smiles from the pastor, Fr. Ed, and the young receptionist, Kim, greeted me. My grief over leaving OLM was soothed by the healing welcome from my new pastor and community. I felt very much like a puppy dog being led around by a spirit of welcome that remains in my soul to this very day.

The greatest example I have of witnessing a "Welcoming Back" is when my father returned to Sicily for the first time after twenty years. Upon arriving in Sicily, the beginning of a "Welcoming Back" like I had never witnessed before began to unfold. Waiting for us at the airport was the family—all thirty of them—grandparents, uncles, aunts, and cousins. When my father's eyes met the eyes of his family, tears and bear hugs began followed by a motorcade of small Italian cars ready to get us back to the family's village without delay. This was only the beginning of witnessing what "Welcoming Back" is like for Sicilians.

The first time my father ventured out of my uncle's apartment into the main street of the village, he could not walk three paces without passionate embraces of old friends and fellow fishermen. They remembered him as though he never left; likewise for him. Mental pictures of that welcoming back

will always be with me. My father came back to America rested and renewed. I returned knowing that my roots beckoned me to be a "people person" as Catholic priest. And to this day, I value the act of welcome as the sign of healthy Christian community.

The sentiment of the Son's Prayer is blatantly lost in our present day menu of entertainment. With reality TV, the media is hijacking our hearts and minds away from the dynamics of genuine welcome. What we watch on television will lead us to believe that the viewing audience is more interested in rejection than welcome.

The "Survivor" series shows one person at a time being voted off the island. That person walks away from the tribe dejected and no longer a welcomed member of the group. Donald Trump gains attention on "The Apprentice" by stating firmly, "You're fired!" Welcoming attitudes in business seem unlikely when such definitive rejection is glamorized and applauded. Accepting Christ as a welcoming teacher seems an uphill battle in a society that is losing its spirit of welcome. Experiencing Christ as welcoming teacher is most relevant for our times. The Welcoming Teacher is not about hiring his disciples for compensation or deciding who lacks the survivor's edge. Our teacher's plan book is spiritually directed to welcoming people deeply into a new experience of God's presence within the everyday anxieties of life.

The image of being yoked to the teacher to carry life's burdens offers a promise of relief. A yoke placed upon the muscular shoulders of oxen keeps them pulling a plow forward. Seemingly undisturbed by the weight of the iron yoke, the oxen's strength does not falter. Making the yoke manageable for the student ensures that all students' shoulders are naturally relaxed and strong enough to step forward with Christ. Like the oxen, being yoked to Christ, the gentle teacher, maximizes the spiritual navigator's "soul strength."

The welcoming yoga teacher is committed to the wholeness of his students. In the yoga world, it is not unusual to hear this word "yoke," particularly when a teacher is striving to provide reassurance and welcome to those new students who come with trepidation into a room full of people they imagine have comparatively greater flexibility to contort and twist their bodies. The word "yoga" comes from the Sanskrit root word "yug" which means to yoke or join. We hope to allay the student's fear by relating that the true experience of yoga is in its yoking or joining together body, mind and spirit through breath. Christ's directive is a gentle, but compelling invitation to follow his example and live the way that he lived to find more ease through life's journey. This is the full intention and potential of a yoga practice for Christians.

Getting people to a state of relaxation is complicated business. As one feels truly welcome, then perhaps, the person opens up to relaxation. Christ's prayer helps to lift away that which makes relaxation nearly impossible. I asked Madelana to share with me what she has learned about teaching people to relax. Teaching relaxation is only one component of teaching yoga. For many, the ultra-high frequency of living in today's fast-paced, instant gratification culture makes relaxation "nearly impossible" as Anthony has said. With our addictive natures being drawn to intensity and production, it is often quite difficult to settle the mind into a pace that allows the body to simply "be" and in many cases, heal. Yoga offers time-tested methods for achieving this goal. For this reason, we will devote part of a later chapter to "Be-attitudinal" relaxation.

Healing Teacher of Wisdom's Gifts

"Wisdom from God" (1 Cor 1:30) describes the gift of Christ for the Corinthian people. To ancient Greeks used to hearing the wisdom of giants like Socrates, Plato and Aristotle, for one person to be called wisdom itself was most unusual. Christ as the heralded representative of "divine wisdom" was a wisdom teacher within the Jewish tradition, not a pagan one. This Jewish wisdom tradition was passed down to Christ from the reservoir of Wisdom Books (Proverbs, Ecclesiastes and the Song of Solomon). Wise sayings "canonizing right ways of living" to popular statements bracketing a "time for everything under the heavens" gave the Wisdom tradition its eternal relevance. Embedded in a mentality that respected the wise sayings of the past, Christ appears to us as the Healing Teacher of Wisdom's gifts. For us, those particular gifts are contained within the wisdom sayings of the Beatitudes.

Wisdom sayings within the oral tradition gave people another standard to live by besides the precepts of the law. The Torah spelled out for them how to behave. On the other hand, ethical behavior motivated by wisdom sayings called people to reflect first and then act.

When I was young, I remember my mother saying, "When are you going to wise up?" "Wising up" meant becoming mature and responsible and not depending on someone to do what I should be doing. Jesus, the wisdom teacher, calls us to wise up which is the core teaching of the Beatitudes. Becoming spiritually mature and responsible within community is the challenge of each Beatitude. Once that maturity is experienced then the reign of God is more apparent than ever.

Jesus—Teacher of Divine Union

The Jewish soul of Jesus is best manifest through the voice of prayer. He began and ended his day by faithfully praying the *Shema:* Hear O Israel: "The Lord is our God; the Lord alone. You shall love the Lord your God with all your heart, and with all your soul, and with all your might" (Dt 6:4-5). By the habitual recital of such a daily prayer, Jesus remained aware of his Divine Father's presence through the course of his day. His daily affairs included constant interaction with his disciples—

students learning valuable lessons about the expansive nature of God's presence (the Kingdom of God)—and how they were to do God's will.

There is no better example of a prayerful Jesus, mindful of the plight of his disciples in the world, than John 17. The entire chapter presents us with a concerned teacher praying for his students. The lengthy prayer teaches us something profound about intimate union with God, something Jesus earnestly desired for his disciples.

One newly-minted grammar school teacher once told me, "I am always thinking about my students, even on weekends." Jesus was that kind of teacher whose mental remembrance of his disciples was not only by mere thought, but also in the context of prayer. To state that Jesus remembered his disciples in prayer is to imply that within his most intimate communication with his Father the disciples enjoyed center stage.

No one has to ask Jesus to remember the disciples in prayer. For this teacher, praying for them is an intrinsic part of being a true teacher. This particular prayer that Jesus prays is the greatest argument for his certification as a yoga teacher, solidly intent on preparing his students for divine union. In the prayer, the disciples are automatically considered to belong to God, "they are yours" (Jn 17:9). "Belonging to God" rejects any notion that places the disciples outside God at any time for any reason. Once you are part of this divine community, your membership is eternal and unconditional. Out of the affirmation and confirmation of belonging to the divine presence, the disciples are invited into a sublime divine oneness, a mutual open-ended bond shared by the Father and Son, "Holy Father, protect them in your name that you have given me, so that they may be one, as we are one" (Jn 17:11). Our yoga teacher wants his students to experience what he has with the Father. The experience of divine union is not exclusively reserved for the Father and Son. Repeating the hope for divine oneness over and over again (Jn 17:20-23), gives the disciples comfort on their spiritual journey. The repetitive, prayerful hope for oneness shows the teacher's patience and persistence.

To see Jesus as yoga teacher is to use our imagination about a teacher's teacher. He is not concerned about getting his students into difficult poses; he is more excited about what the students share after feeling God within their body. Jesus is the Yoga Teacher who instructs the receptive nature of humans about all that is divine. The *"Namaste"* salutation (translated as *"the divine in me honors the divine in you"*) is a common expression for this yoga teacher who never doubts that God's Spirit has taken up residency in every human heart.

Jesus' human nature is a reminder that we all must live in the body we were given. Jesus' divine nature is a reminder that we are not human beings having a spiritual experience, but rather that we are spiritual beings given the divine gift of a human body. In order to optimize our divinity we must optimize our humanity. In order to move closer to our divine nature, we must more fully embrace our human nature. Through the physical and spiritual aspects of yoga, we may become like a new resident in the home of our own body, fully unpacking and living in every room. With the wisdom of the Beatitudes as the prayer we repeat in our hearts and minds, we may begin to infuse our life with the divinity of a man who lived to show us the way.

Chapter 3

Charting Our Course
Skies are Clear and It's Smooth Sailing

SHOW me on the map where we are headed and how long it will take us to get there. **Map reading has always been a favorite pastime of mine. I remember as a child studying maps as if I were Vasco da Gama or Christopher Columbus readying myself for a lengthy journey. Trips to "the shore" as we call the Jersey coastline, are punctuated in my memory from the passenger front seat, holding the map and navigating my mother to our destination. Back at home-base my brother, Jeff, and I eagerly grabbed our bicycles to ride through our neighborhood learning how one street connected to another and finding new ways to make passage from point A to point B. We called it "exploring," and we were truly making new discoveries each time we would ride. I share memories like this with my yoga classes when I want them to resurrect their own childhood memories of discovery.**

Childhood memories escort us back to simpler times when riding a bicycle opened up a whole new neighborhood with new friends. Our earliest independent journeys down or around the block were filled with carefree, childlike wonder. Our present journey's first intention is to bring us back, with adult-like wonder to a biblical beginning when it was just two brand new human beings meandering in a "green world" with a super-creative God.

With Christ as the teaching captain of our ship, we are comfortably seated on board, paperback Bible on our lap opened to the book of Genesis. As we read about Adam and Eve, our reflective journey begins from their pristine home-base, the Garden of Eden. Using the vivid imagery of the body from Genesis, we have the makings for a magical inward journey into the great beyond. Consider yourself as the spiritual navigator of your own inner world as you take your yoga mat and Bible on board to reinvent your spirituality.

Adam and Eve are birthed by God in a garden. Human eyes see paradise for the first time; auditory marvels, our human ears, are drenched in the melodies of pure nature. The many faces of nature, "the face of the deep" and the "face of the waters" meet a human face with a nose at its center. Into the nostrils of that anticipating face moves the life-starting breath of God. The Nobel Prize winner, Desmond Tutu, claims that "God is forever blowing breath into our being." Divine exhalation persists as humanity inhales and exhales divine molecules from eons ago. Though there is no clothing to which a label may be affixed, a divine designer label is imprinted onto these new beings. The entire human project—body, mind, and spirit—is imaged divinely. For too long that divine-image-status eluded its intimate connection to the body. Yoga energizes a new spirituality of the body, one that capitalizes on divine origins.

Naked and unashamed, our first parents experienced each other as prototypes of sacred anatomy. Shame would only come when these free beings violated the innocence of their holy nakedness. At the beginning of practicing yoga, some of that primordial shame lingers as we pass judgment on our appearance and performance. We tend to be unforgiving of our body's imperfections. Our inclusion of the Beatitudes into a yoga practice helps us to return confidently to why we were gifted with a body by God in the first place. Our hang-ups about not having the perfect proportions only weigh us down from discovering the sacred dimensions of the human body "as is" without cosmetic enhancement.

After some time reflecting on our reading of Genesis we decide to stand up on our yoga mat because our sit bones are getting tired. Near our mat we have that new set of binoculars given to us by our favorite single aunt who has traveled the world several times. We pick up those binoculars and gaze back toward Eden as our vessel sails away. We view the home we must leave in order to enter the depth of our spirituality; we have an all-encompassing view of beautiful gardens that feed our soul with soothing sights, sounds and smells. What we see "out there" prompts our second reflection: how the human body is garden-like and home-like at the same time.

As we move away, we are better able to appreciate the comfort of our beloved house and garden and as our magnified view diminishes, we may reminisce about our homes as the haven for our bodies and personal belongings. Our bodies house our less visible, less tangible aspects: emotions, thoughts, spirits, etc. Just as sustaining fire or flood damage can undermine the safety and comfort of our home, failing to care for the body can bring about similar results under very different kinds of circumstances. Illness and injury are reminders of the importance of a healthy body for a comfortable life. The practice of yoga is a fine way to restore and renew us while gaining insight into the correlations between a healthy body and compassionate heart.

Owning and caring for a house is a sizable responsibility. The details of this responsibility are not immediately obvious to a perennial apartment dweller. One of the greatest moments of admiration in my marriage so far, came after I moved into my husband's house and witnessed how well he knows and cares for it. When my husband was away for his firefighting responsibilities, his first question to me on a rainy day was often, "How is the basement?" Before I came to understand home ownership, I was insulted and wondered how he could ask about the basement before he gave sufficient attention to me, his beloved. My attitude was that a little water in the basement wasn't a problem if we got to it eventually. Obviously, I had never owned a house. Here is a bit of history that helped me to grow into my new role as homeowner.

Early one August morning, Chris and I awoke to find water on our first floor. This was alarming, but before I could even engage my brain, he was down in the basement and taking care of the crisis. The furnace shut-off valve had failed and the water flowing through the pipes to the radiators had begun to overflow. The entire basement had a good six inches of water, far above the usual small area that flooded with torrential rainfall. This was truly a mind-boggling experience for me. But my husband knew his house with all its quirks and needs intimately. This, combined with his on-the-job training as a fireman, ensured he could handle such an emergency, and so he turned off the water and began the task of pumping out the basement and discovering the cause. This was one of those "larger-than-life" events that vividly imprint in one's memory. Remembering this life lesson I learned in my new home prompted me to appreciate our home and all the memories it holds.

As we sail on, continuing to glance back and appreciate the glorious colors of our garden set against the blue of the sky, the relationship between home and garden inspires more contemplation for this journey. Just as a house can be likened to our body, the home of our spirit, a garden can be the metaphoric way that we celebrate that body.

Gardens dress up the outside of a home, truly revealing the creative nature of the inner dweller. I consider myself lucky to have a husband who, with decades of landscaping experience, has developed his gift of creativity and appreciation for the beauty that nature can add to a home environment. He puts a great deal of time and love into his garden. Though I generally leave the bulk of this work in his very capable hands, I have been afforded enough time in our garden to appreciate how healing it can be to work in the dirt or "soil" as he calls it.

As I have learned to understand what I "see" when I notice a home's exterior, he has helped me to tap into my own creative instincts. Flowers add color and beauty to the outside of our home. Trees and shrubs provide shade and privacy when appropriately placed and pruned. Grasses add an element of texture to the overall view of the property. Potted plants allow us to decorate the patio, the way that decorative vases and lighting can add interest to an indoor space. The vegetables and fruit that we grow in our garden bring nutrition to our table, and an extra bit of health, since we grow them without pesticides and with the rich soil of our compost piles. All of these aspects of gardening contribute important things to our home. But this all takes a commitment of time. Caring for the garden of the soul also takes commitment, but the rewards are out of this world.

So it is with the body—home of our precious true self. We must learn the skills necessary to care for and make it a structure fit and enjoyable for dwelling. When we eat right, allow time for silence and prayer, engage in satisfying physical pursuits, and share life in community, the rewards of these healthy behaviors shine out in our radiant skin, glowing eyes and positive attitudes. The radiant beauty of our exterior is much like the inviting beauty of a home with a lovingly tended garden.

While housekeeping and gardening take time and attention, contemporary culture promotes immediate gratification. Only the most beautifully appointed homes make it to the magazine pages, disregarding the reality that, for most of us, it takes a lifetime to complete our home's appearance. Demand for perfect lawns and gardens require the use of pesticides, toxic chemicals that ultimately abuse the earth's soil and likely the bodies of those handling them. In one way or another, this desire for a perfect appearance interferes with healthy living. In a similar manner, pursuit of a perfect physical appearance preys on people with insecurities. They are drawn to extreme measures of self-annihilation such as exercise addiction, eating disorders, and plastic surgery, just to name a few. People who endure abuse of any kind are hindered from enjoying the wonder and glory of their body. Like a pesticide intended to alleviate one condition, the abuse infiltrates the garden of the body, mind and spirit with toxic results. When shame spreads and overtakes our positive sense of wonder, we are left with poor body image, negative thinking and decisions made only for appearances' sake. Only with loving acceptance and balanced self-care can we bring our bodies to a radiant glow.

Back from the momentary muse about our beautiful Garden of Eden, we bend our knees and kneel down to pick up our wind-blown Bible that has opened to a Jewish-Christian prayer book called the Psalms. We are not superstitious, but we accept that Psalm 139 is just for us. Driving home the message requires prayer.

> *"For it was you who formed my inward parts; you knit me together in my mother's womb. I praise you, for I am fearfully and wonderfully made."* Ps 139:13-14

The above verses from Psalm 139 are easy for me to understand because my mother graciously crocheted afghans for family and friends, and I was a recipient of her ongoing maternal creativity. Her long hours of tedious work producing these warm coverings rewarded her with great pleasure at the sight of her completed work. When I was doing theological studies in Belgium, one of her "heart-made" afghans kept me warm many a night. Imaging God doing a so-called "feminine activity" like knitting, easily reminds me of my mother crocheting at the kitchen table.

The maternal tone of these psalm verses helps us to pray from a body that speaks to us about God. In other words, the psalmist readily accepts that his/her body talks to us eloquently about God. The idea that the body is simply a "container" is pure slang for the "body conscious" psalmist. Although we constantly engage in self talk, for most of us our body only talks to us when we are in pain. When our reliable back is strained after picking up a heavy object, our back grabs our whole attention. When we reflect on God's hands knitting our cells together in "utero," our innate curiosity about our inner workings, "wonderfully made" by God is awakened.

Just as the psalmist calls us back to our sacred bodily origins, our practice of yoga with the Beatitudes shares the same goal. Living as a stranger in our own skin doesn't do justice to God's handiwork. Only through the proper love and care of our body are we going to be saved from the constant assaults on it. A common crime of modern society is the disrespect of the sacred nature of the human body. This is ritually expressed at the end of a Catholic funeral. The body is incensed as a sign to the community that this body held God's life-giving Spirit; this body was knitted by God in a womb on earth.

American popular culture is obsessed with the body. Only a very few fit the standards of "knock-out" beauty set by *Sports Illustrated* and *Cosmopolitan* magazines. Extreme makeovers coax the candidate into thinking that life really begins for them after they have been fixed by the practitioners of the beauty industry. Their looks and their clothing were inferior before; life begins anew because their outward appearance is changed. The constant barrage of this kind of thinking diminishes the inherent sacred character of the human body.

What are we to believe about our bodies in order to stop this insanity? Stepping into our garden with the Beatitudes and Christ will provide a fresh beginning. We may not leave our garden as an icon of physical beauty, wrinkle free, but we will leave it, aware and awakened to the body as a teacher of spiritual wisdom in imitation of Christ and to the need to be faithful to holy relaxation and bodily peacefulness. All of this will convince us that the body, like Christ, is the true servant of God's indwelling Spirit. Our holy anatomy, discovered through yoga and the Beatitudes, will meet our desire for union with the divine.

Passing another vessel on our left gives us cause to stand up, stretch our bodies and wave hello to our sea-borne neighbors. Standing now becomes the perfect opportunity for one ritual to give rise to another. Steady in the present moment, we await the feelings that come from ritual gesture and words. New insights for a healthy body image are being born at sea. Leaving behind our old body assessments, we take a new look at why God created the human body. Within the Catholic community there is a ritual that maps out body awareness for Sunday worshipers.

Our reverence for the body in Catholic tradition is acknowledged in a ritual from the Rite of Christian Initiation of Adults. At a chosen Sunday Liturgy, those serious about embarking on this new faith journey are welcomed by the community during an ancient rite called *Rite of Acceptance into the Order of*

Catechumens. Part of this ritual focuses on the sacred meaning of the human body for this group of newcomers. During the Rite, the "Signing of the Candidates with the Cross" begins with each godparent tracing the cross on different parts of the candidate's body, beginning with the middle of the forehead:

> N., receive the cross on your forehead. It is Christ himself who now strengthens you with this sign of his love. Learn to know him and follow him.

After this initial signing by the godparent, the "Signing of other senses" takes place. The words and gestures of cross-tracing on the ears, eyes, lips, breast, shoulders, hands and feet signify the "Signing of the Sacred Body."

Worshipers are consistently impressed that the community wants the potential members to know that their entire body is holy from the top of their head to the tips of their toes. For cradle Catholics, the awareness of the sacred nature of the body, empowered by ritual, gives one the ability to see and understand the body anew.

Rite Adapted for Our Journey

Seeing us take a standing position to rise and stretch and greet our passing neighbors on the ship nearby, our yoga-teacher, ship-captain Christ takes the opportunity to invite us to experience this ritual as an initiation to an embodied spirituality. We close our eyes, take a deep breath and stand tall, peacefully expectant as Christ traces a heart symbolically over our entire body. Gentle whisperings, like these below, fall softly:

- Open your ears as the stories of this journey travel to your heart.
- Open wide your eyes to see your body as God sees your body.
- Moisten your lips to express your body's joy as the Beatitudes surf your breath.
- Open your heart like never before to the Spirit's voice within its chambers.

- Roll your shoulders for the placement of a gentle yoke.
- Spread your fingers to hold your divine purpose.
- Spread your toes to walk in a new direction of compassionate love.

For the novices on board, experiencing learning in Catholic Christianity, this ritual serves to identify the body's appreciative role on the road to the baptismal waters. We are not on this Christian journey waiting to be disembodied and ghostlike. Our yearning for physical initiation and acknowledgement is as one who has been longing to be inscribed by Christ.

For those on board who have followed the teachings of Christ deep into the heart of Catholic Christianity, the occurrence of physical being, imprinted with ritual wording, becomes a tangible adventure of spiritual embodiment: an outward expression of an inner truth.

With the blessing and acknowledgment of our bodies, we feel truly ready to take a deeper journey into the Beatitudes. Our curiosity about how they might relate to the ancient art and science of yoga is peaking at this moment, and our willingness to cross the bridge to these ancient worlds of wisdom has been accelerated.

You will be taking a simple yoga journey into the Beatitudes now. Follow the photographs and the instructions for the Short Practice on the foldout pages; keep a playful attitude as you attempt each *asana*. Once you feel comfortable with the *asana*, focus more on the breath just as you did while you were sitting. Then repeat the accompanying Beatitude quietly to yourself, using the reflections to the right of each set of photographs to give you a contemporary application of these ancient wisdom statements.

Come on to your yoga mat and sit in any comfortable position with your spine tall and your breath slow, deep and rhythmic. Close your eyes and allow your mind to begin to unwind as you listen to your breath. By listening with all of your attention, allow your breath to bring you further away from the outside world and gradually more aware of the inner world of the Spirit.

Chapter 4

Heading Out to the Deeper Waters
Finding Spiritual Tools for
Survival on the Journey

℘

THE wind catches our sails and our vessel sprints grace-fully further out to sea. With land no longer visible, we are well into our yogic journey. But as usual, it takes a while for the body and mind to fully unwind and enter the attitude of a spiritual vacation. **As a dear priest friend counseled me before a vacation one year, "You don't take a vacation, the vacation takes you."** We learn this rather quickly when flights are delayed, luggage is lost, or hotel accommodations dis-appoint our expectations. "Spiritual vacation awareness" happens when you've done all your planning efficiently and now must give way to variables outside of you. You suffer the minor inconveniences to allow vacation-time to restore you to the full comfort of your true self.

Beatitudes, Christ and the Practice of Yoga takes us into deeper waters where there are fresh insights. Akin to the vacation anal-ogy, our journey's risk is rewarded in the end by the letting go of our prejudices and fears. Lost luggage is not a concern because what we need is not packed inside our luggage; it is tucked inside us. A survival kit was issued to us the day we were given our magnificent body by God. Our goal is to break open that survival kit with the help of practitioners who under-stand the physical benefits of yoga. Our journey transforms these benefits into spiritual ones for anyone open to meeting Christ through a new venue and to renew one's life with the spiritual wisdom of the Beatitudes.

Nestled within the word *vacation* is the word *vacate*. Vacationing is emptying your life of its usual practices. It's clear to us at this moment that life on this vacation is dramatically different from life back on land. Life on board affords us the time to be quiet with ourselves. Like it or not, we have been given the opportunity to go within and find that voice inside waiting for us to finally pay attention. We ask ourselves, "How will we survive the solitude of this journey?" The answer that resounds from deep within is that our survival depends upon our ability to develop a healthy body and mind—God's explicit desire for us.

Yoga teaches that persistent practice gradually nourishes a body to become both strong and flexible and that the outer reflects the inner. As the mind unlocks, the bindings on the body yield. As the mind becomes stronger and more resilient, the body takes on healthier aspects of strength. Christ supremely modeled the qualities of strength and flexibility each time a person approached him for healing. He stretched forth his "flexible Spirit" to help someone regain strength lost by disease of any kind. On board the yoga boat, he asks that we follow his lead by demanding three things of each of us.

Daily we must work our bodies with *asana* ("aah-sahna") practice to keep our physical health up to the performance of our tasks on board. (The illustrated short practice on the first foldout at the end of the book has been our introduction.) There is ample time to allow for required solitude and quiet to help the mind maintain healthy alertness and keep creative instincts fresh. Finally, with the body working and the mind rested, we must exercise our hearts in the procurement of greater levels of compassion. Each of these practices serves a fundamental purpose of life on board our ship. As a community of shipmates, we do these practices not only for our individual health and well being, but also for the well being and survival of the community.

Having heard us wondering aloud about whether yoga is really worth our time and effort, Christ nods his head approvingly because he sees the physical practice of yoga is beginning to unlock deeper questions. He smiles knowingly when he reminds us that our practice has just begun with easy poses and heartfelt reflections on the Beatitudes.

Christ knows that we are going to want some cold, hard facts about why he wants us to do yoga as part of this journey, so he has given us an assignment to review and discuss Timothy McCall's "Count on Yoga" (*Yoga Journal*, Jan/Feb 2005). The article has been neatly tucked into our lifejackets. Thirty-eight ways are listed as reasons to begin practicing yoga. McCall's catchy titles—rephrased for our purposes—stimulate our own creativity and prompt a discussion about the physical benefits that yoga bestows on its practitioners. Though all 38 are great reasons to do yoga, seven of the 38 speak directly to us about how this yoga practice will underlie our healthy living onboard and off this "Beatitude Boat." We review this article and decide as a community that these therapeutic foundations for doing yoga are also offering us reasons to take this journey out into deeper waters and confront our need for healing and our hidden fears.

Heart and Soul, Ebb and Flow

The cardiovascular system is a powerful pump system that ensures that the fluid of life-blood is continuously moving throughout the body. Smack at the center of this system is the pump—our heart. The heart is a muscular mass about the size of a fist, and it sits in the middle of the chest cavity, slightly more toward the left side. Generally, the term "muscle" conjures up images of those muscles that move bones and give the body its stature and shape, like the biceps and the triceps and the ever-popular abdominals. There are other types of muscles in the body working without any conscious assistance. The heart represents one such type of muscle. The cardiac muscle moves blood through the veins which also do their own kind of mild pumping using another type of muscle called smooth muscle which also does not need any conscious attention to function on our behalf.

I have visited many people in hospitals recovering from "open-heart surgery." Doctors and nurses want to get a patient back on her feet as soon as possible in order to get the blood circulating normally through the body. Follow-up sessions of cardiac rehabilitation abbreviate the time a person feels excluded from the flow of family and work. I experienced my own father stepping anxiously back into the flow of family life after his mitral valve replacement. His speedy recovery restored the flow of family living for his young children by returning our mother back home from long days and nights at a distant hospital. My father remained on disability and became one of the first Mr. Moms when my mother went out into the workplace.

Yoga's promotion of blood flow could be just the restoration needed for a fatigued and listless spiritual heart. Dean Ornish, the famous cardiologist, writes in his book *Love and Survival:* "The real epidemic in our culture is not only physical heart disease, but also what I call emotional and spiritual heart disease." The "pure heart" of the sixth Beatitude is a noble incentive for a renewed flow since it guarantees us a good look at God. Spiritual heart health is just what Christ the teacher ordered for us. Heart-healthy attitudes endorse the order coming from the Master of the Sacred Heart.

Flexible Goods

Many times when I meet beginners in my yoga classes the first caveat they offer is "I am not very flexible; I can't even touch my toes." Though yoga does not require flexibility, it does improve flexibility over time. What I have noticed over the years is that students continue to come back to yoga class because it multiplies good feelings. Even the stiffest, most rigid body can gradually attain greater levels of flexibility simply by committing to practice on a regular

basis. When the tightness of the body is sloughed away, it's almost as if the practitioner has stepped into fresh, suppler skin.

Physical flexibility improves spiritual flexibility. A spiritually flexible person is open to learning new things about the variety of God's Spirit manifested within everyone without exception at every moment. This form of spiritual flexibility is not something we leave at the door before we enter our offices or homes. Cutting off someone in conversation or in traffic because they don't espouse our personal belief system keeps us stiff and inflexible. The instruction Christ our teacher gives us is to stretch further than we think we can go, especially when it means embracing someone different than ourselves. The spiritually flexible become the most advanced students of Christ our yoga teacher.

Weight and See the Benefits

Trimming down is good for our health, but how do we lose the excess baggage that weighs us down spiritually? The "stuff" cramming our insides is the reason we gain those extra pounds. Overeating or under-eating may be a symptom of a spiritual or emotional problem, the kind of problem that has us perpetually searching for the perfect everything: body, relationship, children, home and career. Coming up frustrated when they are not found, such pursuits weigh us down. We need to be lighter and freer. Yoga assists in that intention.

Eating disorders have been described as among the most difficult conditions to rehabilitate because the very substance of the addiction is needed to sustain our lives. Yoga offers ways of dealing with the struggles of eating-related issues. Yoga practice is often based on a physical practice of the body called *asana*. *Asana* practice is posture practice. Sometimes *asana* practice involves moving into and out of postures or moving from one posture into another, always in synch with the breath. When the body is engaged in activity, it is burning calories to fuel that activity. When *asana* practice involves holding one posture steady for many breaths, there is a building of muscle tissue and strength. Since muscle is dynamic tissue, it offers greater calorie burning when you are at rest. Either way, you win!

In addition to all of the movement and muscle productivity, proper breathing and a multitude of breathing techniques offer the body's metabolism a kick-start. Proper breathing alone can have a significant impact on our body weight as we improve the efficiency of our metabolism. Yoga practice can burn some calories and at the same time will lead us to reduce any excess weight. Christ, our yoga teacher, is light on his feet and wants to show us how to be just as light on the inside.

Strength of Spirit

Strong muscles serve to protect the body's joints and help to ward off conditions like arthritis. This is the body's way of stabilizing an unstable situation. When our leg muscles are strong, our backs don't take on the work our legs should be handling. Yoga's offer of flexibility with strength allows our bodies to maintain a suppleness that working out with weights alone cannot offer. The gift of healthy youth is a flexible, pliable, resilient body, mind and spirit. Keeping those qualities while our bodies age is the path to longevity.

Rachel Schaeffer's book *Yoga for Your Spiritual Muscles* gives validity to yoga. Developing our physical muscles strengthens our spiritual muscles. Male teens want to bulk up to impress friends and potential girlfriends. They want to look "buff" in order to feel more self confident, build muscles, and feel better about themselves. Building up our spiritual muscles by working our physical muscles through yoga benefits the true self, as well.

Growing spiritually does not drain us of inner strength; it's about connecting to the strength of compassion, a spiritual muscle for Schaefer. Instead of trying to impress others with a strong physical form; we bond intimately by sharing our joys and sorrows as participants in the circle of the spirit. A circle connected by a common resource—a life-giving dynamic energy. Christ our Yoga teacher rejoices and suffers with us in such an empowering circle.

Worry Transformed

Cortisol has been referred to as the "stress hormone." In conditions of stress, such as a "fight or flight" response, this hormone appears in excess levels in the bloodstream. You'll recognize it as that feeling of panic that does not abate after you have responded to a sudden stimulus. Yoga works at lowering cortisol levels. By halting the sense of emergency that drives the hypothalamus to trigger the mechanisms that alert our body to act quickly, yoga and meditation can significantly quell our reaction to unproductive stressors. Unproductive stressors are those situations where we react urgently, but despite that we can't effect an immediate resolution. By lowering cortisol, yoga can also help with other symptoms of excess stress: major depression, osteoporosis, high blood pressure and insulin resistance, as well as belly-fat accumulation resulting from non-hungry eating habits.

Slight rises in cortisol levels due to "life," place us all in the gallery of "worry warts." Mothers and fathers do some serious worrying about their children's welfare every day; it is encoded within their maternal and paternal instincts. A conscientious parent finds relief in knowing that their child is just fine. For example, when an adolescent son or daughter walks through the front door after a party night with friends, worrying parents literally "breathe a sigh of relief." When the nurse calls from school to say that one's child is complaining of severe abdominal pains, the pain of worry disorients the parents until they see their child and know he or she is being cared for.

Worry interferes with our physical, emotional and spiritual well-being. Yoga and the Beatitudes offer ways of handling our worries with an embodied spirituality.

Christ our captain is like a concerned parent. He knows that we often worry unnecessarily. He realizes that we may get ourselves all "worked up" by trying to synthesize the Beatitudes and yoga perfectly. As you include the Beatitudes with yogic practice, just briefly imagine that Christ comes over to you, places his soft-bronzed arm on your shoulder and looks lovingly into your eyes. No words are exchanged; a sacred silence descends. You feel secure in his sacred touch; his gentle dark eyes generate peace as your breathing slows down and your heart rate decreases. Now you finally feel what it is like to be worry free from the inside out. Christ slowly lifts his arm away, and we journey on having learned another valuable lesson.

Pain Reformed

Richard Rohr, a popular Franciscan preacher and spiritual writer, specifies that the main objective of spirituality is the "transformation of pain." How do we do more than manage our pain? For the most part, we end up repressing painful experiences, transferring our pain onto loved ones, and increasing our pain by wrong choices. Physical pain is met with analgesic prescriptions; other forms of pain send us to therapists and other professionals. According to Timothy McCall, studies have been completed that offer evidence that *yogasana*, meditation or a combination plan reduces pain in people with arthritis, back pain, fibromyalgia, carpal tunnel syndrome, and other chronic conditions. **Over the years of teaching yoga, I have been privileged to know many courageous folks who have chosen to use yoga, meditation and other healing arts to successfully help with these conditions and others.**

Using these methods to alleviate pain puts us in control of our own health and well-being. Knowing what to do to quiet pain that may arise in body or mind is the highest form of health. This can be as simple as knowing which yoga posture to do to alleviate a sinus headache or which series of postures eliminate premenstrual symptoms. Using *pranayama* (breathing exercises) to help with a feeling of sluggishness or depression can put the power of a happy day into our own hands. Searching for ways to alleviate the symptoms of pain is a lifetime process.

For many, the pain they feel is so unbearable they will do anything to relieve it. Heart-break is a pain that can feel unbearable and interminable. **Ministering to bereaved parents I have found that there is no greater pain than when a parent buries their own "flesh and blood." The bereaved parents that I have met through the years are all "working with the pain." For most, this constant, relentless pain ends only at their death. The idea of transforming their pain is an ongoing, daily process of healing with slow, barely perceptible results. The bereaved parents I have encountered on this healing journey are the most spiritual people in the world; their loss has allowed them to be held by the awesome, parental heart of God, making them aware of love and loss at every moment.** Our compassionate teacher, Christ, wants to show us the way to ease pain by surrendering with our tears of mourning to the comfort of God's strong arms.

It's clear to us now that there are more reasons to do yoga than we could have previously imagined. The fact is that it offers many benefits that we will definitely appreciate receiving. Linking yoga to the Beatitudes still challenges the most critical- minded among us, but Christ has assured us that if we put our judgments aside and simply do the practices, we will experience the message and intent of the Beatitudes in our bodies. He even hints at the idea that this ancient practice has a philosophical basis that is not unlike our own belief system. Perhaps if we do this together we will feel better and stronger, happier and less anxious, and that will make life onboard more pleasant. The sky looks a bit darker now and there is word of a storm out at sea. Perhaps we should go below and do a few yoga poses to relax.

Chapter 5

Surviving on the Sea
Mapping the Journey with the *Sutras*

જી

SEVERAL sunsets have passed since we began this journey. We have not seen land for two days. The recent storm has made us more aware of the absence of our loved ones and the comforts of home. Telling time by the cycles of the sun and moon *(ha-tha/sun-moon)* sets an inner rhythm in motion that we have come to call our "inner knowing." Awareness and inner knowing are two senses that yoga reawakens. Rediscovering the spiritual gifts can spark hidden fears, but in the safety of our floating clan, it offers more opportunities for conversation and connection. At times we think we are traveling without a map, but it's certain that our captain knows the way. Christ's face never wrinkles with worry and his brow never shows the strain of fear. We trust that he will guide us safely through the bad weather and high waves, though we can't decide how he remains so peaceful and calm while we feel restless and unsure.

The first time I heard the word "*sutra*" was in a yoga class. The good teacher defined the Sanskrit term as "thread." A mental image arose—my mother threading a needle and sewing a button on a dress shirt. She always had her tin box with multi-colored threads and buttons easily accessible for the next urgently needed repair. A spool of thread often saved the day. Can *sutras* "thread" us back into the garments of the "soul"?

You may already know the *sutras*. Your practice of yoga may have you reading and studying these ancient Eastern spiritual sayings on a daily basis. For our journey to remain faithful to the yogic tradition, we feel it is necessary to show pertinent parallels between the wisdom of the Beatitudes and certain chosen *sutras.*

Thus, one evening, a philosophy teacher on board our humble vessel approached Christ, our yoga teacher, and asked, "Can *sutras* help people understand the Beatitudes better?" Christ, open and receptive to the wisdom of the ages, gently responded, "Threading the Beatitudes together with *sutras* will help us practice yoga and live the Beatitudes evermore gracefully." The questioning teacher leapt for joy; she had always felt the connection, but never dared to ask the question. Katherine had done her homework and came up with the following *sutras* to share with her fellow mates on board. As she offered her rendition of each selected *sutra,* Christ in his most comfortable role of wisdom teacher, initiated a dialogue amongst us, adding his own reflection of how these ancient and wise threads were complemented by similar Christian teachings.

> *I.33—The mind becomes quiet when it cultivates friendliness in the presence of happiness, active compassion in the presence of unhappiness, joy in the presence of virtue, and indifference toward error.*

Happiness and *compassion* are "bosom buddies" on our journey. They seem inseparable to others on board. One fellow traveler thought that *happiness* only traveled or cruised on the Queen Elizabeth II. He thought that taking the "Beatitude Boat" would not be appealing to someone used to the finer things of life. Another mate thought that *compassion* would only show up at hospitals and other health care facilities to remain true to its identity. Why then would happiness and compassion be onboard? The Beatitudes teach a version of happiness paired with compassion. Our yoga practice enlightens us to see this "sacred pair" everywhere.

Since yoga is classically defined as *stilling the fluctuations of the mind,* the practice of yoga concerns itself with observation of the mind's activity while engaging in other aspects of the practice. Since our minds are the master interpreter of our experiences, the way that we think serves to teach us much about the self. Many think of yoga as practices of the body, but the *sutras* tell us this is only a small aspect of practicing yoga. The great cartographer of the yoga world, Patanjali, mapped out the yogic journey in the yoga *sutras* of Patanjali.

Sutra 1.33 indicates the way the mind can remain free and unfettered when it meets with the various personality types that are certainly encountered. Cultivating friendliness in ourselves when we meet someone who is happy may be an easy task, but it is not so easy to behave, as this *sutra* suggests, with active compassion when we meet someone who is unhappy. The *sutra* says that if you are not compassionate to those who are unhappy, then you will not find rest in your own mind. The Beatitudes remind us that when we are mourning, we must accept God to be the supreme "Comforter," but if those we meet have not learned to be compassionate in the face of unhappiness, we may question the veracity of this Beatitude. The Beatitude reassures us that comfort will come from God through all those who profess to be "images of God." The *sutra* is a method for a practice of the individual; the Beatitude takes the individual's rested mind and places it at the service of healthy communal living.

When you meet with someone who is virtuous, do feelings of doubt or jealously arise? The *sutras* teach us that if we cultivate the quality of joy when we encounter someone with good qualities, our own life will be enhanced. **My time spent with Anthony in the challenge of being first-time writers of a book with a deadline in the midst of a busy career, a new marriage and a house undergoing renovations is a joyful event because he is a gentle man with a good heart and a Christ-like compassion for others.**

But it is not uncommon in the workplace for a co-worker to be jealous of our good qualities and see them as a threat. Every day people try to undermine those who practice virtue in order to advance their own interests. The Beatitudes teach that those who are persecuted for righteousness' sake will receive the kingdom of heaven. Heaven's reward may not come in the form of a promotion, though we may see this as a real need. Heaven's reward comes in a feeling of deep comfort with yourself so that you can be accountable for doing your part.

"Do you see how these two sets of wisdom practices can work together to create a greater sense of wholeness in our community?" Christ asked. Mary quickly responded back, "So that means, when my friends poke fun at me for coming on this journey, remaining indifferent means being open to forgiving their erroneous impressions of such a journey." He replied, "The overt evidence is in the peacefulness of your mind. Your compassionate presence will win them over for the next time we set sail."

Cultivating these qualities in the self is a means to becoming "Beatitudinal." Our hope is to create a peaceful environment where each person can feel whole. By threading the *sutras* together with the Beatitudes, we can gain a slightly deeper insight into the message of Christ.

II.2—*The intent is to gradually attain the state of contemplation and diminish the causes of suffering.*

"I hardly pray, forget contemplation. I've had my fair share of suffering in life. Nothing reduces my suffering, and I take it like a MAN." Our female passengers felt sorry for Joe, one of the few males besides Christ who booked the "Beatitudinal Boat." Joe booked this trip because of his new girlfriend. He grew up Catholic and she was a student of yoga. One day they got into a heated argument about who prays better. His girlfriend insisted that she prays better now that she goes to yoga classes. Joe asserted that the only place you really pray is in a church. Stubborn and resistant, Joe is starting to let go into the experience. He shares firm beliefs about what he is hearing because of his keen mind and strong will, not easily changed by any yoga teacher, even if that teacher happens to be Christ himself. In any event, Joe is lovingly accepted for being honest. Someone Joe has taken a shine to (maybe a threat to his new girlfriend) remarks, "Joe, you're keeping your eyes closed longer at the end of our daily practice. Watch out! That 'contemplation jazz' just happens unexpectedly."

Christ chimed in, "Do you all remember that first downward facing dog pose I asked you to do?" Grunts and laughter arose from amongst us. We thought about those seconds that felt like minutes as we held this posture on hands and feet with our hips lifted in the air. "My hands wanted to slip out from under me and my shoulders were screaming as I waited for you to let me come down," said Sally. "I couldn't believe you when you said this was a pose of rest." Just days later, we have all come to love or at least appreciate this pose, since we have developed the understanding of how to use our legs better and to notice when we are getting lazy and not putting forth our full effort. "So this is the way that you gradually learn to focus on one thing and that concentration becomes a deeper state of awareness called contemplation," said Christ. "And when you develop this ability to an adept level, you will discover yourself focusing better off your yoga mat as well." This got us to thinking about how, when we started with this pose we hated it; we found it so difficult and it made us suffer. Only days later, we've developed the ability to practice this pose by concentrating on our bodies and suffering less and less each time we encounter it. "Hmmm, I see how you are using this yoga to help us develop better skills for life," said Joe.

> II.29—*The eight limbs of yoga are: respect toward others, self-restraint, posture, breath control, detaching at will from the senses, concentration, meditation, and contemplation.*

Yoga can be compared to a tree with eight limbs or branches. Each of the eight limbs is a fundamental component to climbing this tree to its top. Not surprisingly it all begins with respect toward others. The Beatitudes teach us a new way to view each other that seems to stand in stark contrast to the conventional view of people. Christ taught the Beatitudes to ask us to elevate our vision to a higher aspiration. The eight limbs of yoga clearly show that if all we do is move our bodies into postures, we are not doing yoga. We must see others through eyes that are guided by an open mind. If we disrespect the poor and suffering out on the street and judge them as being less for having less, we are no more doing yoga than we are being a "*beatitudinal* Christian." There is just no compromise on this issue.

> II.30—*The principles of respect for others include nonviolence, truth, honesty, moderation, and non-covetousness.*

Patanjali understood human nature; he recognized the need for more instruction on "yoga means respecting others." The yoga *sutras*, therefore, define what it means to respect others. We call them the *yamas* and the true meaning is to look at our attitude not only toward others, but also toward our surroundings. If you disregard the environment by dumping toxins into the water supply, you need to look at the things that shape that attitude. By the same token, if your behavior causes harm to another, whether by words or weapons, you must take a good honest look at this. One's political positions may need revision; one's office strategies often require reevaluation, all because Beatitudes and *sutras* have been seriously introduced into your mind and heart. Our attitude toward our environment will show up in our attitude toward others . . . eventually. The yoga practice is the process that affords a good and honest look at that attitude.

> II.35—*Around one who is solidly established in nonviolence, hostility disappears.*

We all know that part of going on any journey is "wanting to get away from it all." Dr. Andrew Weil advises his readers to "fast from the news when on retreat or on vacation." Our evening news is replete with violent incidents; it is frightening for those who watch it and even more frightening for those who live just blocks away from the crime. No one in their right mind wants violence of any kind to happen in real life; yet we flock to our theaters, paying way too much, to see actors and actresses act out brutal, violent scenes for our entertainment and enjoyment. Descriptions of graphic violence in mild and extreme scenes do not dissuade us from inviting our friends. How then does the value of nonviolence, promoted in these *sutras* and spoken of as peacemaking in the Beatitudes, become less a word and more a style of being and doing? Have we become numb to the detrimental effects of violence whether in movies or video games?

Take the examples of Gandhi and Dr. Nelson Mandela. These two peacemakers were solidly established in non-violence. They chose their paths based on righteousness' sake despite the persecution they experienced. But they were solidly established in non-violence. The path to peace is not a short-cut, nor is it a "cake-walk." There is no war that can bring peace, and that extends to war in foreign countries and gang wars in our neighborhoods or in our prisons. The commitment required to establish peace takes as much energy as the expenditure of dollars to build bombs, but peacemaking means that we must communicate, not detonate.

III.30—Perfect concentration on the throat frees one from hunger and thirst.

On board our Beatitudinal Boat are sufficient rations for all. However, one day Christ our yoga teacher wanted to experiment with another spiritual practice commonly found in all religious traditions: fasting. Upon hearing that all on board would be invited not to a feast but to a fast, reservations about the whole journey resurfaced. Christ, as we have learned, never recommends anything to his students without having experienced the benefits and burdens first. So Christ reminds us about the time he spent in the desert fasting for forty days. Then he set the time for fasting to last from Friday evening to Saturday evening. Those who were accustomed to some form of fasting accepted this spiritual practice while those who anticipated every meal had serious doubts.

Because Christ timed the fast to coincide with Katherine's reading of *sutra,* the throat became a center of concentration each time yoga postures and meditation were scheduled. Saturday night came quicker than expected and after our fast, the buzz on board about what was heard besides growling stomachs were insights about hungering and thirsting for righteousness and desiring to act according to God's will. Through the shared experience of a disciplined fast an inner fulfillment was born.

III.34—Perfect concentration on the heart reveals the contents of the mind.

Concentration on the throat moves to concentration on the heart. Looking into one's heart is like opening a glass door to one's mind in the *sutras.* The Beatitudes are "heart-openers" first because they move into the mind as new guidelines for living in community. The *sutras* seek to explain the state of being when clarity of mind joins with the dynamics of the pure heart.

In the distance, the chant could be heard, "Happy are the pure of heart, for they shall see God."

Taking the time to look into the heart is not a luxury. Many marriages fail because neither party has concentrated on "what is going on inside their hearts." The wedding culture overtakes young, engaged couples and leaves their minds spinning about a host of things that move their concentration away from the unity of their hearts. **Prior to a wedding, I try my best to get engaged couples to put aside the checklist of things they must do before the big day. Their minds are geared in overdrive about many things from flowers to**

favors, things that do not give them a moment to concentrate on their hearts.

All of the Beatitudes help us to turn away from insignificant things like acquiring items that end up in piles in our basements and garages, like hoarding the latest technology in our living rooms, and like scolding our spouses when they fail to pick up after themselves. The Beatitudes blend nicely with this *sutra* because it emphasizes that what is really "important" is not always what is going on in our physical, material world. Concentrating on what is going on in the heart shifts our focus away from the quality of things to the quality of relationships.

> *III.50—Spiritual liberation comes when we renounce even omniscience and omnipotence, and when the origin of personal causes of suffering is destroyed.*

Dr. Martin Luther King exclaimed, "Free, free at last!" That passionate sentiment spurred on the civil rights movement in the sixties. Liberation from the shackles of prejudice and fear began a new life for our sisters and brothers of color. That kind of social liberation is a lesson for personal spiritual liberation. We are imprisoned when we think we have all the answers, a presumption that intoxicates us with power. Unlocking the cell door does not depend on a corrections officer; it depends on our willingness to be humble before spiritual knowledge and wisdom. The Beatitudes in unison with this *sutra* liberate us from all kinds of prejudice about groups different from us. Experiencing the freedom Dr. King preached is spiritual liberation; one that unifies a humble heart with a healthy body.

As Katherine read the *sutras* aloud and Christ offered his interpretations, a lively discussion arose with others chiming in to share what they felt about connections to the Beatitudes. One eager person said, "That word contemplation reminds me of deep prayer, some sort of mystical rapport with the divine. I think the Beatitudes are intended to give us a new way of experiencing the divine within a community of people with basic needs." Heads were nodding with approval. Another offered, "There seems to be a deepening that happens with the practice of yoga. Isn't our establishment in nonviolence the first step to a real plan for peacemaking? I can see how hostility on the inside only creates all kinds of hostility on the outside." As we looked around at that group we could see that this discussion was beginning to form a true community. For the first time all week, we could see how communicating our thoughts and feelings was creating something powerful and healing.

When people begin to find common ground through wisdom traditions, great things are liable to happen. The *sutras* and the Beatitudes comment on "hunger and thirst." The *sutras* seek freedom from the "hunger and thirst," the Beatitudes spiritualize the physical need and direct it to slaking one's thirst and satiating one's hunger in a gratifying relationship with God.

Beatitudes, Christ and the Practice of Yoga is a sacred log on land and sea. The entries are invitations for your mind to think anew, your soul to be placated by wise sayings and the wisdom of Spirit, your body to stretch into poses that become embodied prayers.

Chapter 6

Sermon on the Mat
Flowing into Practice with Christ and Yoga

WHEN Christ addressed a crowd, he captivated them. Whether they agreed or even understood him had little to do with how well he held their attention. Everything about the way he presented himself and the way he interacted with them just flowed. Perhaps it was his body language: welcoming, inviting, at ease with himself and comfortable with his knowledge as well as with his mission to dispense that knowledge. Perhaps it was the way he engaged them with stories, or parables as they were called at that time. Christ's use of the parable was a simple method for presenting his deeply spiritual teachings that could be shared and understood by a vast group of people of diverse ages and walks of life. Or maybe it was his timelessness: being able to speak to people of any age and address their fears, doubts and concerns regardless of his age. At 12 he spoke to adults and awed them with his knowledge; at 30 he healed countless sick people. He invited the meek and encouraged the oppressed; he held judgment for only those who elevated themselves above others. These qualities make for a master yoga teacher whose message is enticing to all students.

When master yoga teacher, John Friend, speaks to a hall filled with yoga practitioners, a sense of welcome pervades his body language, his tone of voice and his message. He begins by inviting everyone to come closer together. His message is woven together with stories from his life and the underlying wisdom of the ancient yoga scriptures so that these ideas can be applied to our lives. We are instructed to consider our own story as we listen to his weaving of the ancient and modern, and we are invited

to use these meaningful memories or intentions to give extraordinary power to our physical practice of yoga *asana*. It is artful to watch him work, but what is most apparent is that he enjoys himself, his students and the art of yoga. This is the way that Christ taught. He enjoyed himself, his disciples and his subject matter.

Good yoga classes have all of the elements of good sermons, but with one difference: the message is applied to the physical movement of the body. The message is given a tangible form as we apply its meaning in the body. Breathing and moving in postures causes the entire body to come into rhythm, a process called *entrainment*. As the body becomes entrained, it becomes more yielding and receptive and that condition allows messages to gain entry into our deeper self. Breathing and moving or holding a yoga posture while the mind is contemplating a Beatitude allows the cells' receptive condition to receive that message. In this way, we learn something new through the body, bypassing the conscious mind and inserting the new experience into the subconscious mind. To simplify, since everything that exists is some form of energy, it's like baking a cake with the ingredients being our energy and the energy of the Beatitudes; the preparation process is the *asana* and our breath. The result is a sumptuous, satisfying and nurturing slice of dessert.

This practice is a physical one involving movement or, at times, stillness, and always the breath. Through it we are remembering the words of the Beatitudes or learning them for the first time, but what is being transmitted even beyond the words are the meanings. By opening the body and all of its cells to the Beatitudes' message, we absorb the state of being intended by Christ when he taught the Beatitudes. It is the experience of a Beatitudinal practice, not for the mind to comprehend, but for the soul to revel in. Remember the words of Neil Donald Walsh, "you are not a human doing, you are a human being."

So as you prepare to take this practice onto your own personal mat, prepare to stop doing and start being. Prepare to relax your cognitive mind and awaken your sensate being. Allow your breath to be a continuous reminder of your burgeoning light and then place yourself on the deck of Christ's boat surrounded by friends who support your spirit's entry into the community of a Beatitudinal lifestyle. Learning the Beatitudes, not by embracing them mentally but by experiencing them physically while simultaneously contemplating their meaning, without undue attachment to a result, is exactly what we believe Christ would want for each of you. Practice your yoga; live your Christianity by fully opening yourself to the core of Christ's spiritual teaching: The Beatitudes.

In order to fully benefit from a practice modified by the Beatitudes, a sampling of background material is necessary. Historical, religious, and socio-economic considerations in a Jewish culture weigh in on the original meaning of each Beatitude. We balance ourselves with one leg on a yoga mat and one stretched tightly back to the Holy Land of the first century.

> *Blessed are you who are poor, for yours is the kingdom of God.* (Lk 6:20)
>
> *Blessed are the poor in spirit, for theirs is the kingdom of heaven.* (Mt5:3)

A huge reality is staring at Jesus before he teaches the Beatitudes from the sky-laden heights of a scenic mountain (Mt 5:1) or the grassy ground level of a plain (Lk 6:17): large crowds of sick people seeking attention, healing and wholeness. They came to him overburdened by bodily afflictions, worn down by travel and evil spirits (demons) thought to be the culprits of their plight. Reaching out to this vast throng of broken people becomes the healing prelude to the teacher's lesson plan for happiness within the Kingdom of Heaven *(the respectful reference to God and God's presence)*.

Labeled poor in the first century carried a considerable social stigma. There were levels of poverty. Some barely survived each day by getting what they needed. The absolutely downtrodden begged in the marketplaces. "Survival by hand-out" was automatically disdained and ignored by the wealthy and fortunate. Your poor-person status said you owned nothing, ruled nothing, and wielded power over no one. You were lost in the masses and considered to be a failure, like "all the rest of them." Claiming a right to anything was taboo; your destiny was one of sheer want and persistent despair.

For a rabbi like Jesus to casually bequeath the Kingdom of Heaven to the undeserving masses boggled the entitlement mentality of the time. Noble people knew how to manage kingdoms, should *they* not also govern the kingdom of God? Jesus freely entrusts the full experience of his Father's kingdom to those who claim no power, position, or prestige. The social hierarchy is turned upside down; the elite are at the bottom and the poor are at the top in Christ's new social order (*Jesus' Plan for a New World*, Richard Rohr).

Matthew's rewording of the first Beatitude to include the poor *in spirit* broadens the eligibility requirement for active membership in the Kingdom of Heaven. Luke's Beatitude strictly refers to the poor as described in the previous paragraphs. Matthew expands the meaning of poor beyond economics to encompass all who feel the need for the deeper experience of the spiritual life. "Poor in spirit" crosses all artificial boundaries between poor and wealthy and accepts everyone to be spiritually powerless to some degree. All the children of God are "poor in spirit" without exception. For those that accept such a spiritual reality the experience of heaven is close at hand.

The Kingdom of Heaven is like a fine pearl according to Matthew's Gospel (Mt 13:45-46). For us in the 21st century, Luke would have the poor wearing a fine string of pearls around their neck. Matthew would have everyone concealing that precious pearl deep within the cave of the soul.

↪

Blessed are those who mourn, for they will be comforted.
(Mt5:4)
Blessed are you who weep now, for you will laugh.
(Lk6:21)

Isaiah was a major prophet for the ancient Israelites. Most of the time, prophets were summarily ignored, even as they spoke candidly on behalf of God and his best intentions for all his people. Biblical scholars describe Hebrew prophets as "mouthpieces" of God in good times and bad. On the mega-tragic occasion of the Temple's destruction (587 BC), Isaiah boldly writes, "comfort all who mourn; to provide for those who mourn in Zion—to give them a garland instead of ashes, the oil of gladness instead of mourning, the mantle of praise instead of a faint spirit"(Is 61:2-3). Christ's Beatitude of consolation is spoken from the heart of a devout Jew who never forgot the catastrophic pain of the Temple's destruction.

Who comforts? The grammar of this Beatitude contains a divine passive: "for they *will be* comforted." Although the name of God is not mentioned for religious reasons; using the divine name would assume a casual, disrespectful approach to the Holy. There was no greater loss for God's chosen people than to cope with life without temple sacrifice and the commandments solemnly sheltered in the Ark of the Covenant. Matthew's Beatitude remembers the "mourners" of a temple lying in ashes. In memory of those "garlanded mourners," the prophetic teacher continues assuring people that their losses are not intended to be handled in loneliness and privacy; God is the supreme "company" of all wounded hearts within his kingdom.

Sin causes mourning. That belief is professed in Psalm 38:18, "I confess my iniquity; I am sorry for my sin." Another translation reads, "I acknowledge my guilt: I grieve over my sin." Sin was loss. The ancient Israelites felt just as horrible about sin as they felt about other major losses. Losing the temple edifice meant losing God in some concrete, visible way. Offending God with sin meant losing the blessings of God. Mourning God and his blessings could only be definitively resolved by God as unconditional comforter.

This Beatitude's meaning recalled the memories of great loss and disillusionment. However, it did not stop there. The Teacher's agenda included the inheritance of the Kingdom. Thus, for those who mourn, for those who are poor, for those who think they have lost everything imaginable, this Teacher gives a new future. The hope of the Beatitudes is for the times when you feel depressed, thinking you have lost everything— persons, property, God—that God faithfully extends a helping presence into the future.

Luke's parallel to this Beatitude is "Blessed are you who weep now, for you will laugh." Luke's humorous hope tempers the outward emotion of grief. Tears and wailing are transformed into unanticipated laughter. In the next chapter (Lk 7:11-17), the same positive attitude of the Beatitude has the compassionate Christ encouraging the widow of Nain, "Do not weep." Christ is starting the process of transformation for the widow and leading her to the beginning of a new life with her once deceased son. Grieving is transformed for those who feast in his Kingdom. At that feast of "rich food and well-aged wines (Is 25:6), God holds the tissues as "he wipes away the tears from all faces" (Is 25:8).

᠆

Blessed are the meek (gentle), for they will inherit the land.   *(Mt 5:5)*

Moses and Jesus share a common personality trait—meekness. "And the man Moses was very meek beyond all the men that were on the earth" (Num 12:3). Jesus' prayer to the Father discloses his closeness to Moses, ". . . for I am gentle and humble in heart" (Mt 11:29). Moses, the first lawgiver, paves the ascent up the mountain for Jesus to become the new lawgiver. Moses gave the Ten Commandments to the people of Israel, not from leadership based on arrogance and pride, but from his humility. In imitation of Moses, Jesus presents a new set of commandments, the Beatitudes, from that same trait of overlooked and undervalued meekness.

Meekness and being poor are interchangeable in the ancient world. The poor owned nothing. They worked long and hard on the landowner's property. Rights to the land originated from God and were inherited by the "right people." To accept that these rights would be granted to the meek was quite unconventional. Unless you prayed Psalm 37:11 seriously, "But the meek shall inherit the land, and delight themselves in abundant prosperity," this Beatitude is disconcerting and absurd.

The Land, to this day, is a major symbol of Jewish identity. Sabbath, food, nation, temple and the Land are essentials to Jewish life and history. Guarding and protecting the Land is first. The meek might not have what is needed for national security, considering they could be poor. In the end, the meek symbolize a new system where the "least expected" take center stage before those on the top. "They will inherit the Land" from God not because of their placement in society but because God rewards humble human hearts. Understanding why God chooses the meek makes this Beatitude spiritually challenging for all generations.

⤷

Blessed are those who hunger and thirst for righteousness, for they will be filled.　　　　　(Mt 5:6)
Blessed are you who are hungry now, for you will be filled.　　　　　(Lk6:21)

Biblical righteousness is applauded in Matthew's Jewish world. Pious Jews sang of "righteousness" in the Psalms each time they dutifully fulfilled the divine will. Outward proof of this submission rested firmly on the meticulous practice of the Law. A zealous, law-centered Israelite took great pride in a proper relationship with God; righteousness was their just claim to religious expectations dictated by the Law.

Satisfying the devout Jew's desire for "right relationship" with God is encouraged by the psalmist who sings away his troubles in the desert with the lyrics, ". . . for he satisfies the thirsty, and the hungry he fills with good things" (Ps 107:9). Matthew borrows this imagery and attaches it to the quest for righteousness. Connecting hunger and thirst to righteousness consoles the offender of the law; it gives the disciple a new way of thinking. The pure intention behind the law is just as important as acting upon the law. With that in mind, the disciple is guaranteed that the faithful God of the covenant will grant happiness to all who hunger and thirst for food and drink as though they were hungering and thirsting for God.

Luke's advocacy for the poor (*the anawim*) reappears. The poor are physically hungry; they are not to be excluded from what God generously gives to his people. The bounty of the harvest must be shared in order to please God. They are considered to be happy in their hunger, for God wills their satisfaction. Luke's poor are first in the Kingdom of Heaven. Their tears are wiped away; their hunger satisfied; they are the winners of a great reward in heaven—part of that reward commences on earth.

⌒

Blessed are the merciful, for they will receive mercy.

(*Mt 5:7*)

The God of the Hebrew Scriptures possesses the attribute of mercy. This divine form of mercy is also called "compassion" and "steadfast love." Only the Divine One possessed such an attribute until this Beatitude. All who would like to humbly imitate this divine attribute are invited to do so in anticipation of their happiness within the Kingdom of God.

Sharing in "mercy" invites willing disciples to a new experience of God. This Beatitude ushers disciples into the compassionate workings of the Kingdom of God. The ancient law is not the final say and arbitrator of one's future with God. In this Kingdom, the practice of mercy is valued as the new "Law of the Land."

"Obtaining mercy" is rediscovering the image of God upon us. This Beatitude coaxes us to trust that being created in the divine image and likeness makes acting compassionately easy. Our truest self desires to give and receive compassion; in the mutual sharing of compassion, affirmation is forthcoming from the Divine.

Blessed are the pure in heart, for they will see God.

(Mt 5:8)

Peak spiritual experiences in the Bible often occur on mountains. This Beatitude is taught on the mount, but its inspirational background is found in response to a practical question about climbing the holy mountain of Zion to the temple. "Who shall ascend the hill of the Lord? And who shall stand in his holy place? Those who have clean hands and pure hearts, who do not lift up their souls to what is false and do not swear deceitfully" (Ps 24:3-4). The excited pilgrim was getting nearer to the place of all their dreams, the temple. Fulfillment of the dream assumed that ritual and ethical purity were practiced in preparation for such a holy visit. *Mikvahs* (Jewish ritual baths) along the journey kept the pilgrim consistently in the state of ritual purity.

For Matthew, ritual purity was extremely important, however, it was not the end-all solution for participation in God's kingdom. There was something more that did not necessarily need the purifying waters of a bath. A "pure heart" was read only by God without external verification by ritual.

"Seeing God" was the awesome reward of a pure heart. This kind of seeing was not a matter of human eyes but of eyes peeking out of a transparent, pure heart. The quest to see God was a real desire for pilgrims on their way to Jerusalem. The Beatitude suggests that a pilgrimage is not needed; one need not travel to see God. At any moment, without having to go on pilgrimage, the opportunity for a full-scale, divine experience is possible. Traditionally, the limestone temple rises on the mount; one can ascend to God from the temple within, without seeing the limestone in the distance.

⌔

> *Blessed are the peacemakers, for they will be called children of God.*   (Mt 5:9)

Kings and angels received the honorary title, "son of God." Oil poured over the king's head, anointed him as "son of God." Governing the people as a "son of God" wielded heavenly power on earth. Earthly subjects bowed down in reverence before a monarch crowned by God. Heavenly angels stationed at the throne of God, sent on missions to earth, possessed the divine status with their royal counterparts. Lastly, faithful descendants of Abraham attained the status of "child of God" by agreeing to be the people of Yahweh.

Jesus' fidelity to the Torah and practice of covenantal love with Yahweh merited him a distinguished status as a chosen child of God. Jesus was the great example of "father like son." The early Christians called Jesus *the* "Son of God" as a way of exalting his name because of his resurrection. Appearing to his disciples after his resurrection, "Jesus came and stood among them and said, 'Peace be with you' " (Jn 20:19). The Risen Christ grants peace to make all his followers—peacemakers.

Peacemakers are not peace-lovers in Scripture. Granting peace is a divine function. Taking up the role of peacemaker invites people into a divine function. The Beatitudes present the opportunity to be like God in regards to compassion and to act like God in regards to peacemaking. In all of the Hebrew and Christian Scriptures, only in this Beatitude is the term "peacemaker" used. To unite peacemaking and one's placement in the kingdom is unique.

⤳

Blessed are those who are persecuted for righteousness'
sake, for theirs is the kingdom of heaven.   (Mt 5:10)

The word righteousness reappears in this Beatitude. Already we know how this term is more about faithful relationship than exact moral behavior and certitude. Those who decide to follow these new rules of the kingdom may be rejected by others. There will be a price to pay for acting according to the Beatitudes. Those who endure persecution and rejection in a worldly kingdom are "VIPS" in the Kingdom of Heaven.

Missionaries for Christ and his new way of living were harassed by those unwilling to put aside the old ways. The message of the Beatitudes wasn't welcomed with open arms in many quarters. Die-hard traditionalists balked at the idea of having to adopt a new standard of living, why not just let the old way of thinking and acting remain as is?

The "Kingdom of Heaven" again is given to those least eligible according to the rules of the past. Those who stick to their convictions will be rewarded and congratulated for their solid commitment to the community charter of the Kingdom of God (all the Beatitudes).

⤳

Blessed are you when people revile you and persecute you
and utter all kinds of evil against you falsely on my

account. Rejoice and be glad, for your reward is great in
heaven, for in the same way they persecuted the prophets
who were before you.   *(Mt 5:11-12)*

The promise of a reward for living according to the
Beatitudes gives motivation to the disciples. Adopting a new
way of living is not for the faint-hearted, but the pure-hearted.
Following the commandments of the new lawgiver doesn't
come without risk and possibly persecution. This is an orienta-
tion into a new school that has an old school foundation.

The message of the Beatitudes is prophetic, thus the fate of
the prophets may also be encountered by the disciples. Christ,
as a prophet, was rejected and vindicated with the resurrection.
Living the Beatitudes makes prophets out of disciples. Living
the Beatitudes and practicing yoga may push us forward into a
prophetic life that will have its days of rejection coupled by an
inner happiness.

Understanding the meaning of the Beatitudes then, in first
century terms, grounds all our contemporary interpretations.
Yoga on this journey is a spiritual practice acting like a set of
keys to new doors that are often locked. Once you have the
right set of keys in hand then entry is possible. The more we
retrieve the original meaning of the Beatitudes, the more confidently we will be opening doors to an elaborate feast on board
the Beatitudinal boat.

**In the Long Practice of Beatitude Yoga on the second foldout,
breathe with focus as you perform new postures. Feel the bodily
power of the Beatitudes revealed through the postures. Reflect upon
the inspirational verse. Encounter Christ in a new way, away from
thoughts and ideas, grounded in your sacred body, speaking a new
language of love to you through yoga.**

Chapter 7

Telling Tales of the Journey

ॐ

CHRIST invited us to talk. "It's time to share with our group what you are feeling, thinking and learning. I hope our experiences on the Beatitude Boat have freed you to speak your mind and heart honestly." The group is eager to share now. At the beginning of the journey, some were biting their tongues, a few were uncertain about this journey while others were bubbling with enthusiasm about what this new experience would offer.

Our sojourners settle into a circle on deck, some cross-legged in Lotus Position. Feeling less critical and guarded now, their practice of yoga and the safety of this compassionate community have freed them to disclose their personal experiences of yoga and the Beatitudes.

Mary spoke first. With strong conviction she stated that there is a direct connection between the way yoga feels in her body and the meaning of the Beatitudes. Her "touchy-feely" personality was the result of being raised in a family who lived by the adage, "people will remember not what you said, but how you made them feel." She *felt* the Beatitudes for the first time and was amazed at how different feeling them is from memorizing them from a book. She described this difference by saying that she had become aware of "viewing her fellow human beings as souls first and bodies with personalities after that." A teacher herself, she recalled Howard Gardner's "Multiple Intelligences Theory" and placed her experience under his category of Bodily Kinesthetic Intelligence.

"Yes," said Kelly, "I had a powerful experience in *savasana* (corpse pose) of feeling Christ by my side; I don't remember ever being that peaceful. And having that sensation opened my mind to the possibility that my Catholic religion is not just about obligation, but about applying general, caring wisdom into our daily lives." Everyone in the circle started nodding his or her head.

James strongly agreed with Kelly and proceeded to tell a sad tale of why, to this day, he feels alienated from organized religion. He believes in a Higher Power, a God of some kind, but was badly hurt by clergy persons along the way. James is gay and has never felt welcomed or accepted in his local parish. He felt that he could not do anything to change who he truly was before God. This experience of yoga and the Beatitudes helped him to go beyond the prejudice he experienced and remember why he feels drawn to Christ and his message. James' feelings attracted many compassionate ears in the group.

Joan, a curious spiritual navigator, also felt a correlation between faith and yoga. Her tale was a happier one. She is that consummate spiritual navigator who bobs her head in and out of new classes and experiences all the time. She is a Baby Boomer unafraid to march under the banner of a "spiritual seeker generation." This initial experience of yoga and Beatitudes has her seriously thinking about starting a regular practice of yoga at the local studio. This new way of learning the meaning of the Beatitudes was a long stretch from boring religious education classes that had her daydreaming most of the time. She revealed, in a not-so-joking manner, that her fantasy was "to have the pews removed from her church and see that they were replaced with yoga mats!"

A healthy dialogue was now in progress. Everyone remained respectful and waited their turn to tell what had gone on for them since embarking on the Beatitude Boat. "Finally, something has me connecting my body and soul," Sue interjected, waiting for reactions from the group. She continued, "Combining yoga practice with my religious beliefs will surely deepen my practice of both." Louis contributed that he now understands better what people mean when they tell him that he has "a soul, a spiritual dimension." He admitted to his past ignorance and his acceptance that certain things were just above his average intelligence. The practice of yoga woven into the Beatitudes opened Sue and Louis to how the body and soul can live in harmony together. They, too, are part of a generation that may be leaving behind unhealthy religious traditions and finding their spirituality in unison with others.

Katherine spoke up about what happened when she told many of her yoga teacher colleagues that she was preparing to come on this nautical journey combining yoga with Christ's teachings. The reactions were surprising to her! "It prompted some of the most meaningful conversations I have had in a very long time," she said.

Other voices continued to chime in. Mary Ellen expressed her opinion that "yoga is one way to God." Joseph, a timid chap, pulled out his new German-made harmonica and began to play a tune to everyone's surprise! At the end, he passionately exclaimed, "That's my way to God!" Joseph went on to tell the following tale. "I grew up in a comfortable home with loving parents and my grandparents lived a few houses away on the same block. After school we would visit them and munch on Grandma's homemade biscotti. Life was relatively easy during those early years. Holidays came and went. Summers were spent at the shore; everything was going great. Then all hell broke loose in high school. It was a wise-guy senior who really lured me down the wrong path. He invited me to his home one day after school, and he showed me things I had never seen before: paraphernalia of a drug world. He dared me to try something with him; looking back now I was a damn fool for doing it. I am one of those people who got hooked on the first experience. My drug addiction grew through high school, and was full blown in college. One day when I could not take my lying and deceitful behavior any longer, I sought help from the youth minister of my local parish. I felt more at ease with her than with the parish priests. She cared; she wanted to help; she advised working the Twelve-Step Program; and she became my spiritual mentor. Then one day I mistakenly walked in to the wrong class at my local health club; it was a yoga class. It was during the relaxation pose at the end that all the inner work with the Twelve-Step Program started to make sense to me. I felt the Higher Power in my body. I returned to that class weekly. Yoga has complimented my spiritual work with the Twelve-Step Program. Whenever I feel God's presence, I pull my harmonica out of my pocket and play. People are stunned, and then I tell them why.

As the tales became more intense and personal, bonding occurred. Isabella was tapping her foot as Joseph played his harmonica. Bright-eyed and charming, she is ready to tell what was churning inside her heart. Isabella was the quintessential caregiver in the group. She lived with her widowed mother. She was successful at work, she had multiple marriage opportunities but felt totally responsible for her mother's needs. She enjoyed the living arrangements, but longed to have her own spouse and family. In any case, she was generally happy to share her mother's elder years. Isabella always felt the desire to live a more Christian life. Her friends recognized that she was already Christ-like in so many ways. She humbly deflected those compliments. Coming on this journey has opened her up to the core of Christian life through the Beatitudes. She, like her fellow spiritual navigators, is in awe of God, has experienced Christian faith and wants her yoga practice to renew the awe and rekindle her Christian call.

As the sharing continued, Mary Lou simply stated, "I feel relaxed! I feel calmness, openness, loving acceptance and connection to everyone on this boat." A resounding, affirmative sigh came from all around the circle. Christ asked if we believed that relaxation is a sacred experience. This idea struck the group as a curious one. Since stressful lives have people running in all directions with little time for relaxation, the idea of relaxation being sacred didn't seem so far-fetched. They just never thought about it in that way.

There was a general consensus that yoga and the Beatitudes instilled a peaceful, calming effect—an effect not easily felt rushing from subway to high-rise office buildings. For the yoga practitioners in the group, some of that peace had crept in on occasion in *Savasana* or corpse pose, the final posture in every yoga class. For Christian, first-time yoga practitioners, there was the common belief that their faith practice never provided them with such a deep and profound rest. Their religious experience was laden with rules and regulations that caused apprehension and consternation instead of inner tranquility. Finally, they experienced what they had been hungering for—inner peace and deep rest. The combination of Christ, yoga and Christ's most powerful teaching, the Beatitudes, catalyzed this transformative response.

"Are you ready for some R & R? This is going to be a new experience of yoga *asanas* and breathing *(pranayama)* that will certainly leave you feeling rested and rejuvenated. So far we have focused on practices that incorporate movement and breath and ways to both strengthen and stretch the outer body. Today's practice is going to be an experience in what is called restorative yoga. I like to call it 'sacred relaxation.' Restorative yoga strengthens and opens the inner body, the core," Christ said.

The group was not sure how to respond but all agreed that so far this journey had been full of good surprises. Everyone turned to look at Katherine, the group's resident yoga teacher, for some indication of whether this was going to be good, but she was not showing any reaction. Collectively, they decided to embrace this unexpected turn of events and practice "going with the flow."

The main instruction that Christ gave as we embarked upon this new yoga experience was that we should be extra mindful of our breath since it would provide clues to how comfortable and restful we are. "If the breath becomes rough or shallow," Christ instructed, "it is certain that you are not easeful in the posture. Be sure to change your props or your body's position with care and awareness so that you can remain in the posture for a longer time with ease. That is the secret to restorative yoga," he said. "Oh just one more thing about your breath: always breathe through your nostrils with full, deep breaths unless I guide you to specifically do something else."

For your own practice, you may want to start by choosing one or two of the *asanas* from the Restorative Practice on the third foldout in order to develop a level of comfort with all the props and set up required. Once your body is truly comfortable, absorbing the message of the Beatitudes through the breath and the variety of postures will become easier and easier.

"Well *that* was a different experience," said Joe after we had returned to upright, seated positions from the final supported *Savasana*. "That is something I could do every week, just like going to church!" he said. Most of the group was speechless, seeming almost too relaxed to expend the energy that speaking would require, but for Joe this was exactly what the proverbial doctor ordered. His usually cynical mind seemed to be somehow quieted and soothed by this deeply restful practice of yoga and breath. Christ was hip to the state of introspection that restorative yoga can impart, so he did not rush us to interact. He encouraged us to sit in this new kind of silence and share the stillness together.

Slowly the other members of the group began to stir again. "How did you receive the Beatitudes this time?" Christ asked. Easily reflective, no one was quick to answer, but when we did it seemed we unanimously felt this practice offered yet another way to digest the meaning of these guidelines. Kelly, previously eager to speak up, had to force herself to break the placid silence: "Again I felt that strong sense of Christ's companionship. It was just so remarkable to me; I felt like you were touching my leg," she said to Christ. "You know the one that I broke in that skiing accident. It hasn't felt the same since that event and I can't get over how the sense of your touch made it feel completely healed." Christ just smiled. No, he didn't touch her leg, not in the way that she had imagined anyhow.

After a few more moments of silence had passed, Joseph revealed that he could never sit still for that long and he was surprised that he found it so comfortable to remain in some of the positions for more than a few minutes. One of the residual effects, that he had noticed after so many years of drug use, was that his mind was so active that he had to keep his body moving in order to keep his mind sated. "I tried this restorative stuff in the past, but I just couldn't sit still," he said. "Being able to do this kind of yoga practice tells me that I have made some definite changes over the past couple of years." Christ reminded the group that change is a sign of life. "We are always changing, as long as we are alive. Yoga practice will help you to measure those changes."

Christ announced that tomorrow they would sit in the circle again and imagine what could be next? Most could not wait to do another practice guided by the Beatitudes; others were wondering how we could bring what we had experienced to a greater population. Would the Church embrace this new way of "speaking" to people—accepting yoga and the Beatitudes as one dialect in a new body language of faith?

Chapter 8

Sitting by the Water's Edge
A Compassionate Landing

𝒫𝒶

THE aftereffects of our restorative yoga practice stayed with us the next morning. We felt very bonded, having cried together as we listened to the stories of our shipmates' grave difficulties in life. We held each other in that emotional connection with precious tenderness. We still believe that it was the combination of our masterful teacher, his subject matter and the physicality of our practice that created this magical connection of love.

Christ sat down to breakfast with his students as was his custom, "... Come and have breakfast" (Jn 21:12). He observed his divinely relaxed students politely asking for what looked like butter, but was the new, popular spread for your morning toast. *Smart Balance* tastes like butter, but promises to be healthier for your heart. Whoever came up with the name has the right idea; keeping a *balance* is a *smart* thing to do. Why not start satisfying our desire for dietary balance at the breakfast nook after practicing one of our illustrated yoga sequences?

Spiritual balance is not an easy matter of spreading something on a piece of toast. Heavy schedules tip our scales into *workaholism*. We work long hours to the detriment of our personal lives. A sincere desire to improve family quality of life leaves us exhausted when we spend our meager, leftover time with our families. We are spread too thin. How is spiritual balance attained in the midst of an unbalanced world?

Our journey's purpose has been to bring the whole person into balance, but the playing field of life is tilted and routinely knocks us off kilter. The sacred combination of yoga and the

Beatitudes will keep us steady and stable.

The Christ that we encountered on our yoga journey is not dogma-centered; he is divine-experience-centered. He is the Teacher of Divine Union. Our goal is to engender a union and harmony with God so that we can live our lives with more soul than ego. By experiencing the meaning of the Beatitudes on a yoga mat, we are inspired to live the Beatitudes in our daily lives. The union we celebrate with the Divine is the ultimate goal of all spiritual and religious traditions. We are meant to experience God's intimate closeness during our earthly lives. Father Thomas Keating says that God is "closer than our thinking and breathing." When we experience this union during our lifetime, we will be readily familiar with the deeper divine union that lovingly awaits us in the next.

Paul's Second Letter to the Corinthians, particularly 2 Cor 4:8-10, places our union with the Divine firmly in Christ.

> We are afflicted in every way, but not crushed; perplexed but not driven to despair; persecuted but not abandoned; struck down but not destroyed; always carrying about in the body the death of Jesus, so that the life of Jesus may also be made visible in our body.

Beatitudes, Christ and the Practice of Yoga challenges us to face all the problems of life with new purpose and fresh vision. Difficulties do not dissolve magically because of our newfound spiritual journey. Harassment for thinking and feeling with the Beatitudes is inevitable; persecution for being merciful and compassionate may cause us great pain. Nevertheless, there is a keener sense of the dying and rising within a "yoga-treated" body as we mature in the likeness of Christ. *Beatitudes, Christ and the Practice of Yoga* joyfully celebrates our rising to new life as we become fully aware and awakened to Christ's joy.

A New Friendship and Respect for Christ as a Yoga Teacher

Making new friends and letting go of some friends is part of life. We share this journey with new friends and with a teacher who convincingly taught his original students, "No one has greater love than this, to lay down one's life for one's friends. You are my friends, if you do what I command you" (Jn 15:13-14). Our commandments on this journey are the Beatitudes. They are not mandates from a stern authority, but guidance from a gentle man who wore his divinity like an Irish Setter wears his golden coat. We have gracefully accepted the idea of blending our body's wisdom with the wisdom of the Beatitudes. Our efforts are not in vain; we are meeting new friends and understand better through firsthand experience why our teacher is called the Healing Teacher of Wisdom's Gifts.

Wisdom and friendship are linked in the Book of Wisdom. "She is a breath of the power of God . . . And in every generation she passes into holy souls and makes them friends of God, and prophets" (Wis 7:25, 27). Some of the breaths we have inhaled and exhaled have been part of "power-wisdom breaths;" they could not be any less. Those breaths have traveled on the wisdom of the Beatitudes and may have us speaking up like prophets, catching our breath, saying something we know deep down is in unison with our body wisdom, the wisdom of the Beatitudes, and our commitment to our new cherished experience with a faithful friend who died on a cross for living the Beatitudes 24/7.

After breakfast, we walk above board to breathe in the sun's warmth caressing our skin. Today we feel so much more able to appreciate the beauty of being alive. Before us is the most glorious sight that our eyes could ever take in! The most vivid display of color and scent, and the most profound feelings of joy explode in our heart as our eyes delight in seeing our home!

Having lost full awareness of time, we realize that our journey is almost complete as we approach the shoreline at the Garden of Eden. Simultaneously, we feel a touch of sadness knowing this journey is coming to its end. More than anything we want to know that we can take what we have learned and practice it on our own.

Christ senses our joy coupled with sadness and reminds us of how these emotions are two sides of the same coin. In his usual fashion, he comforts us and reminds us that there is one more experience yet to be enjoyed. His reminder serves to demonstrate to us how easy it is to move out of the present moment and lose our inner balance—a great teaching that we want so desperately to absorb. He instructs us to take our yoga mats and a blanket off the vessel and set them up on the beach. The final expression of this creative journey will be a guided relaxation.

Guided Relaxation

(Record the following for private use, or have a friend read it slowly for group practice.)

Now on shore and relaxed in our favorite position of *Savasana*, the sound of Christ's voice begins to relax us and promise us a safe way to experience peace. If we just keep listening to his words and allowing his gentleness in, we will finally be safe to let go to deep stillness.

⌐

Sit or lie on your back comfortably. Wiggle your fingers and toes as you settle in to relaxation. Take several deep breaths into your belly fully relaxing any tension there. Close your eyes and bring awareness to your body while you breathe deeply. Exhale tension from the lower back. Continue to breathe with awareness. As you exhale, imagine any tightness or tension in the upper back and shoulders is melting away. Release your shoulders away from your ears with every breath. Smooth and relax the forehead and the brow and move the tongue softening it away from the upper and lower palates. Imagine, as your tongue relaxes and your jaw unhinges, that all the tension and fatigue is draining out of your entire body. As you relax, allow any outside noise that you may hear to be a reminder to you to breathe and go deeper. Very good.

Now, use your imagination to step out of your body and see yourself here at rest. How do you appear to yourself? Let the image of your body help you to see what parts you can further relax and, as you exhale, let go and sink deeper into a heavy feeling of rest and peace. Allow your thoughts to pass away and let relaxation spread through your entire being.

Now as you view your body at rest, use your imagination to see or feel me holding you like a protective, loving parent cradling a child. Relax into my warm, loving arms and release your body's weight fully and completely. You have permission to be heavy, let go and be held. As you let go and your body is enveloped by my gentle love, relax your mind and allow your thoughts to turn to the sense of peace that is seeping into your body. Good, very good.

Now envision yourself walking side by side with me. It's okay if you don't see an image; just allow yourself to feel the feelings you can imagine having in my abundant presence. See or feel our two energies walking in a place of beauty. It can be real or imagined. As you walk, allow yourself to tell me your grief or sadness. As you reveal these feelings to me, notice that your body is relaxing more as you unburden yourself and hear my words: Blessed are those who mourn, they shall be comforted. As you hear these words, imagine my arms holding you, one hand on your heart and the other on top of your head. Let go of your grief or sadness and relax in the comfort of this loving peace. If you need to stop, sit and relax a moment, allow yourself to do that and take comfort in that pause. Take a deep breath now, relax and envision our walk continuing.

As we continue on tell me of the poverty in your heart or the weakness in your spirit. You are free to share this pain with no fear of repercussions. As you share these feelings, hear the voice coming back to you: *How blessed are the poor in spirit, the kingdom of heaven is theirs.* Let your doubts and hesitations be washed away and absorb the fullness of this loving moment. Breathe deeply and relax. If you need to stop and rest a moment longer before walking on, take that time.

Continuing to walk on now, appreciate the beauty that is around you in this magical heaven that you have envisioned. Notice any sights or smells or sounds, and as you do, envision yourself pausing to drink in the fullness of this experience with all of your senses.

As our conversation continues, speak of your desire for a world of justice, a world where upright behavior is valued and rewarded in kind. And as the reply comes back to you, imagine a new world where the table is overflowing with a banquet of vividly colorful, delicious delights. *Blessed are those who hunger and thirst for uprightness, they shall have their fill.* As these words resound in your mind, allow your senses to be filled with the joy of gratitude and abundance.

Now in your mind's eye, picture the perfect place to sit and relax for a bit. As we walk together toward this spot, speak of the ways you have tried to practice goodness and love and compassion, but have perhaps been mistreated or misunderstood or downtrodden. Feel my gentle hand cup your shoulder and as you sit down, let my words penetrate your ears and soothe your heart: *Blessed are the gentle, they shall have the earth as inheritance, and blessed are the merciful, for they will be shown mercy.* Now sense the stable earth beneath your seat and the gentle arm around your shoulder and let go of your worries and fears. Know that you are loved. Know that your compassion is returned, your gentleness recorded and your mercifulness rewarded right here, right now in this feeling of peace. Breathe and relax and fully enjoy these sensations.

Now allow yourself to sit in comforting silence with me. After a bit, speak of the attempts you have made to create peace, tell of your persistence and commitment to that process. Share your travails in the pursuit of justice and the ways that you have suffered persecution. And as you say these words, allow your whole being to remember who is hearing your pain. Remember how I suffered, was persecuted and still persisted in the quest for peace and allow your heart to be humbled when my reply comes: *Blessed are the peacemakers, they shall be recognized as children of God, and blessed are those who are persecuted in the cause of uprightness, the kingdom of heaven is theirs.* Continue to make peace and see the good in others, for this will purify your heart. When you are abused and falsehoods are spoken of you as you endeavor to live as I did, remember the way the prophets before you were treated and know you are in good company with your gentle, peaceful, humble heart.

At that, let your body and mind be filled with peace. Relax deeply into this peace and imagine the inner quiet begins to expand outward and becomes a sensation and an experience of embodied quietness. Your flesh and muscles have softened their tight grip; your bones feel heavy, sinking into the earth's support; your mind's boundaries have expanded and virtually disappeared; your heart empty and open now, ready to receive and give without the frustration of attachment. These are qualities that you can be refreshed by and that you can employ to restore meaning and intention to your life.

Call your mind to a scene in your life that has previously challenged you, but now see yourself in this scene feeling as peaceful and relaxed as you are experiencing yourself right now. Breathe into that feeling and that image so the two can be yoked in the cells of your body and the memory of your heart. Now see this new you in the old situation, and imagine a new way of behaving based on your embodiment of the Beatitudes. See yourself and feel yourself fully resolved to behave and believe a new truth. Breathe into this new vision, this new behavior and the new sensations that will follow.

Now relax again and let it all go. See us sitting together where we last were in this beautiful, serene location. Taking each other by the hand for a moment, let's stand now and embrace. You have permission to receive from that embrace whatever quality you most deeply desire to be restored and made whole. You have permission to allow that contact to strengthen and fortify you for your journey back into this life. So linger in the feeling of that touch, knowing that we will part now, each of us to do our own work, each of us having given and received from this experience.

As you turn, see yourself walking away. As we part, carry that feeling of love deep in the core of your being. Breathe into that center spot and allow that feeling of love to warm and enlighten you there. As you breathe deeper into your own center, feel the thread that connects us both, and let this thread generate a warm feeling that radiates like a light getting brighter, shining its beacon to illuminate your path. Feel your skin glowing and your whole essence radiating. Trust that you have all you need within to walk this path of love.

Now remember all of the imagery, all of the sensations, all of your senses fully recharged, take 3 deep breaths and slowly, gently stretch and return to this glorious spot on the shores of your home. Return to this present moment in time.

↩

Slowly we roused ourselves and eventually we sat up, one by one. At that moment, sitting comfortably on the beach, Isabella noticed a colored bottle had washed up on shore. At first sight her environmentalist sensitivities kicked in, cursing inwardly anyone who would be so careless as to toss a bottle overboard. Examining the see-through bottle closely, she discovered there was a yellowed scroll rolled up inside. Her long slender fingers reached in and pulled out a sea-battered scroll. She called everyone over and to her surprise read out loud the following:

Dear Beloved Ones,

You have arrived safely back on land. Do you feel closer to me? I have always been very close to you. For some odd reason, a contrived distance has been foolishly created between us by certain philosophers, theologians, and religious authorities of every stripe. You have gotten to know my son, in a new way. I am so honored that you have used Yoga—an inspiration I gave thousands of years ago in India, for those who desired a deeper union with me—to know the core of my son's teaching, the Beatitudes.

Continue on your journey now, having let go of any apprehension and fear. Rest secure in my love. Please know that I am passionate about an intimate union with you beyond your thoughts and imagination. Through the sacred gift of your body, our delightful experiences together will be more frequent on and off the mat.

Namaste. I salute the Divine in you, for you and I are one.

Forever your Friend and Lover,
God

Bibliography

Books

Bouanchaud, Bernard. *The Essence of Yoga*. Portland: Rudra Press, 1997.

Crosby, Michael H. *Spirituality of the Beatitudes*. New York: Orbis Books, 2005.

Hamm, Dennis. *The Beatitudes in Context*. Wilmington: Michael Glazier Inc., 1990.

Hirschi, Gertrud. *Mudras: Yoga in Your Hands*. York Beach: Samuel Weiser, Inc., 2000.

Mowry LaCugna, Catherine. *God For Us*. New York: Harper Collins Publishers, 1991.

Nouwen, Henri J.M. *The Return of the Prodigal Son*. New York: Doubleday Image, 1992.

Ornish, Dean. *Love & Survival*. New York: Harper Collins Publishers, 1998.

Rohr, Richard. *Jesus' Plan for a New World*. Cincinnati: St. Anthony Messenger Press, 1996.

Ryan, Thomas. *Prayer of Heart & Body*. Mahwah: Paulist Press, 1995.

Schaeffer, Rachel. *Yoga for Your Spiritual Muscles*. Wheaton: Theosophical Publishing House, 1998.

Journals

McCall, Timothy. "Count on Yoga" *Yoga Journal*, February, 2005.

Ryan, Thomas. "Christ and/or Aquarius?" *America*, March 24, 2003.

CD

Brooks, Douglas. *"Currents of Grace: The Philosophical Foundations of* Anusara *Yoga, Vol. 1"* Spring, 2001. www.anusara.com

OTHER BOOKS OF INTEREST

THE SPIRITUAL SPA

Getting Away without Going Away

Mary Kavanagh Sherry

"At this 'spa' we can learn how to spiritually relax and shut out the voices in our heads."

—**From the Author's Introduction**

No. RP 745/04 ISBN 1-878718-99-1   **$9.95**

CHANGING HABITS

The Caregiver's Total Workout

Debbie Mandel

"...presents an innovative program for good health and happiness: Activity Alleviates Anxiety. Debbie Mandel will help you find the balance between giving and receiving to transform stress into strength."

—**Deepak Chopra, M.D.**

No. RP 742/04 ISBN 1-878718-98-3   **$9.95**

LOVING YOURSELF FOR GOD'S SAKE

Adolfo Quezada

This exquisite book of meditations gently directs the reader to see the gift of self in an entirely new and beautiful light. It presents a spirituality of self-love not based on narcissism, but as a response to the divine invitation to self-nurturing.

No. RP 720/04 ISBN 1-878718-35-5   **$5.95**

A PARTY OF ONE

Meditations for Those Who Live Alone

Joni Woelfel

Using each day's brief reflection, probing question and pertinent quote by Adolfo Quezada, this book will comfort and empower those living alone to take ownership of their life, confident of being guided and upheld by God.

No. RP 744/04 ISBN 1-933066-01-6   **$5.95**

OTHER BOOKS OF INTEREST

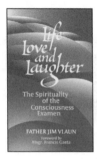

LIFE, LOVE AND LAUGHTER
The Spirituality of the Consciousness Examen
Father Jim Vlaun

"Within only a few pages, you know you're in the company of a truly good man, someone with a big heart whose feet are firmly on the ground . . . There is so much simple, shining wisdom in this book." —*William J,. O'Malley, S.J.*

No. RP 113/04 ISBN 1-878718-43-6 **$7.95**

HEART PEACE
Embracing Life's Adversities
Adolfo Quezada

"This is one of the most authentic books I have ever read on the gut-wrenching conditions that cause or lead to human suffering. . . . His book is a gift, allowing others to be the beneficiaries of his spiritual journey." —*Antoinette Bosco*

No. RP 117/04 ISBN 1-878718-52-5 **$9.95**

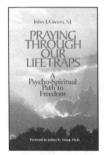

PRAYING THROUGH OUR LIFETRAPS
A Psycho-Spiritual Path to Freedom
John J. Cecero, S.J.

"John Cecero's unique book can be read not only as a primer on lifetrap therapy and practice but as a spiritual guide to finding God in all things."

—*Joseph R. Novello, M.D.*

No. RP 164/04 ISBN 1-878718-70-3 **$9.95**

GRACE NOTES
Embracing the Joy of Christ in a Broken World
Lorraine V. Murray

". . . will help you to see what we should be able to see naturally, but for some reason it takes grace to recognize grace! Her book is well named."

—*Fr. Richard Rohr, O.F.M.*

No. RP 154/04 ISBN 1-878718-69-X **$9.95**

Additional Titles Published by Resurrection Press, a Catholic Book Publishing Imprint

A Rachel Rosary *Larry Kupferman*	$4.50
A Season in the South *Marci Alborghetti*	$10.95
Blessings All Around *Dolores Leckey*	$8.95
Catholic Is Wonderful *Mitch Finley*	$4.95
Discernment *Chris Aridas*	$8.95
Edge of Greatness *Joni Woelfel*	$9.95
Feasts of Life *Jim Vlaun*	$12.95
Grace Notes *Lorraine Murray*	$9.95
Healing through the Mass *Robert DeGrandis, SSJ*	$9.95
Healing Your Grief *Ruthann Williams, OP*	$7.95
Heart Peace *Adolfo Quezada*	$9.95
How Shall We Become Holy? *Mary Best*	$6.95
How Shall We Celebrate? *Lorraine Murray*	$6.95
How Shall We Pray? *James Gaffney*	$5.95
The Joy of Being an Altar Server *Joseph Champlin*	$5.95
The Joy of Being a Bereavement Minister *Nancy Stout*	$5.95
The Joy of Being a Catechist *Gloria Durka*	$4.95
The Joy of Being a Eucharistic Minister *Mitch Finley*	$5.95
The Joy of Being a Lector *Mitch Finley*	$5.95
The Joy of Being an Usher *Gretchen Hailer, RSHM*	$5.95
The Joy of Marriage Preparation *McDonough/Marinelli*	$5.95
The Joy of Music Ministry *J.M. Talbot*	$6.95
The Joy of Praying the Psalms *Nancy de Flon*	$5.95
The Joy of Praying the Rosary *James McNamara*	$5.95
The Joy of Preaching *Rod Damico*	$6.95
The Joy of Teaching *Joanmarie Smith*	$5.95
The Joy of Worshiping Together *Rod Damico*	$5.95
Lessons for Living from the 23rd Psalm *Victor Parachin*	$6.95
Lights in the Darkness *Ave Clark, O.P.*	$8.95
Loving Yourself for God's Sake *Adolfo Quezada*	$5.95
Magnetized by God *Robert E. Lauder*	$8.95
Meditations for Survivors of Suicide *Joni Woelfel*	$8.95
Mercy Flows *Rod Damico*	$9.95
Mother Teresa *Eugene Palumbo, S.D.B.*	$5.95
Mourning Sickness *Keith Smith*	$8.95
Our Grounds for Hope *Fulton J. Sheen*	$7.95
Personally Speaking *Jim Lisante*	$8.95
Power of One *Jim Lisante*	$9.95
Praying the Lord's Prayer with Mary *Muto/vanKaam*	$8.95
5-Minute Miracles *Linda Schubert*	$4.95
Sabbath Moments *Adolfo Quezada*	$6.95
Season of New Beginnings *Mitch Finley*	$4.95
Sometimes I Haven't Got a Prayer *Mary Sherry*	$8.95
St. Katharine Drexel *Daniel McSheffery*	$12.95
What He Did for Love *Francis X. Gaeta*	$5.95
Woman Soul *Pat Duffy, OP*	$7.95
You Are My Beloved *Mitch Finley*	$10.95

For a free catalog call 1-800-892-6657
www.catholicbookpublishing.com